HAZEL
A REDDISH
BROWN NUT

HAZEL
A REDDISH BROWN NUT

HAZEL LEWIS

MOUNT VERNON
PUBLISHING

Privately published in 2024.

First Edition

Mount Vernon branding used under license from Mount Vernon Publishing Group Ltd,
71-75 Shelton Street, Covent Garden, London, WC2H 9JQ.

ISBN: 978-1-917064-91-0

A CIP catalogue record for this book is available from the British Library.

Cover design and typeset by Leslie Priestley.

Printed and bound by Ingram.

For my granddaughter
Catherine Grace

ACKNOWLEDGEMENTS

I COULDN'T HAVE STARTED or completed this book without the cajoling and patience of my daughter, Sally, and for putting in more commas than I thought possible. And for Daniel doing the family tree, although Sally reckons her acknowledgement should be in a bigger type as she put up with me more.

And Mabel, my cat, for waking me up at 5am over the past few weeks when I was able to recall most of my forgotten memories.

INTRODUCTION

IT SEEMS INEVITABLE that even on the day I was born football would play its part in my life. It was a Saturday morning, 17 January 1948 that I started to make my move but things were moving slowly and my Dad was driving my Mum mad. This was due to the fact that my Dad, Harry, had been in a Japanese Prisoner of War camp for nearly four years and, due to the poor diet given to prisoners, he had been worried that he would never be able to father children. As a result of him pacing up and down, my Mum insisted he go to the football. Spurs beat Cardiff 2-1 that day and I have the match programme.

I arrived at approximately 7.30pm that evening. ♠

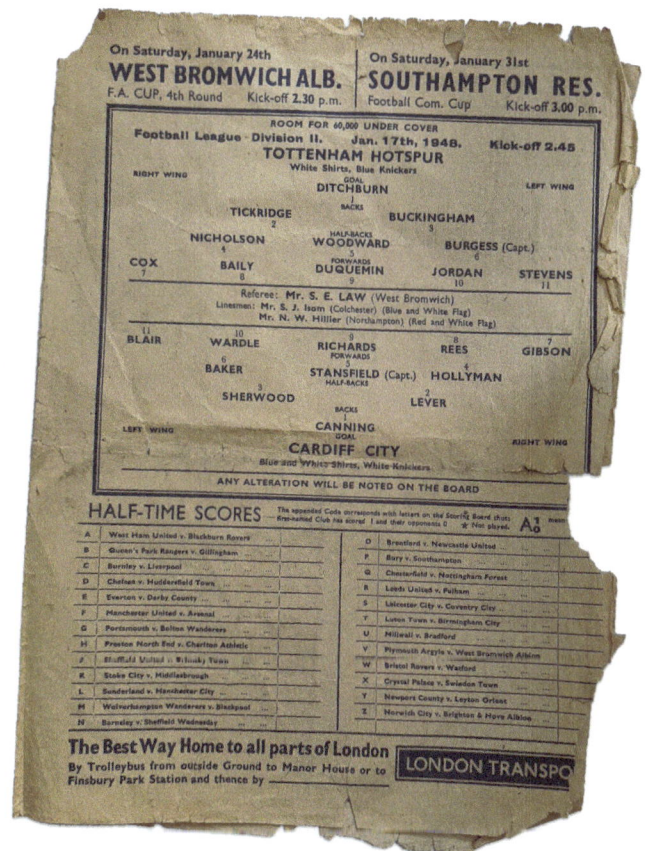

Matchday programme
Tottenham Hotspur vs Cardiff City, 1948.

GROWING UP
IN THE EAST END

I heard a saying on a television programme recently which summed up life in the East End. "There's things I don't know how to want because I knew I could never have them".

MUM AND DAD'S FAMILY both lived in the same street so must have met shortly after his return from Japan, as they were married on the 12 January 1946. There's an old saying, "Marry in haste, repent at leisure" and I think Mum repented for a very long time.

Mum, Honor Lillian Ivy Lee, was a kind and easy-going lady, always willing to help others. I'm pretty

Mum and Dad wedding 12 January 1946.
Back row (left to right) Uncle George (Dad's brother in law) Grandad Harry Goss, Nan Christine Goss, Grandad Jim and Nan Grace. Front row (left to right) cousin Barbara, Mum, Dad and aunt Pearl. Two older bridesmaids unknown.

Mum and Dad c. 1945.

sure there are a few people out there that still owe her sixpence.

During the war she worked as a nursing aide and did fire watching.

She had been a bookkeeper most of her life, working for a printing company for many years. Her last job was in the finance department for City University.

She loved most sports, it's probably where I get it from. I remember her taking Daniel and a friend to the Oval when he was in junior school. When Sky Sports started broadcasting, her front room was often filled with Daniel and several friends watching cricket. I also remember driving to her house at 3am to watch a Formula 1 Grand Prix.

My Dad, Harry Charles Percy Goss, was a complex man, a kind of Jekyll and Hyde, and from what I can gather he didn't have much of a relationship with his Mum resulting in him joining the Royal Engineers 13 months before his eighteenth birthday, 18 being the legal age for enlisting. He had two brothers, Malcolm

and another brother I knew nothing about, who got killed by a Japanese fighter plane that bombed and sunk the submarine he served on, and a sister Phyllis.

He joined the Royal Engineers and after enlisting was posted to Hong Kong but was captured by the Japanese on Christmas Day 1941. When he was released he weighed six stone. When they first got married, Mum would have to stand back from the bed if she had to wake my Dad as he would try to hit out as a result of his nightmare time in the Japanese prisoner of war camp.

After the war, his father, Harry, who was a master plasterer got my Dad a plastering job working on the "White Buildings" in Old Bethnal Green Road. From there his other jobs included working at the American Embassy (from where I got lots of pretty dresses), fruit and veg salesman at Covent Garden and Spitalfields Market. He never ever spoke about his early life and I don't know much about my paternal grandparents other than their names, Harry and Christine (nee Curtis) Goss. He was quite a selfish man and very authoritarian at home, although out of the house he was everyone's friend. And he raised his voice quite often.

My Dad was a good drunk and family Christmas' could be quite entertaining. One Christmas, after indulging in too much cherry brandy, he suffered an upset stomach (that's putting it lightly) but instead of putting Germolene on the affected body part he mistakenly picked up a tube of Deep Heat. Mum came home from work to find him straddling the side of the bath to soothe that part of his body.

For the first 18 months of my life we lived with my maternal Nan and Grandad, Grace (nee Wood) and James Lee, in their house at 27 Cordova Road, London, E3. I remember there being a bathroom but no inside toilet and using the outside toilet was very challenging, especially in the winter. And the toilet paper was old newspaper torn up in squares and stuck on a hook next to the toilet. Instead, at night we would use a chamber pot and empty it in the morning. We used to call them "gazunder" because it goes under the bed.

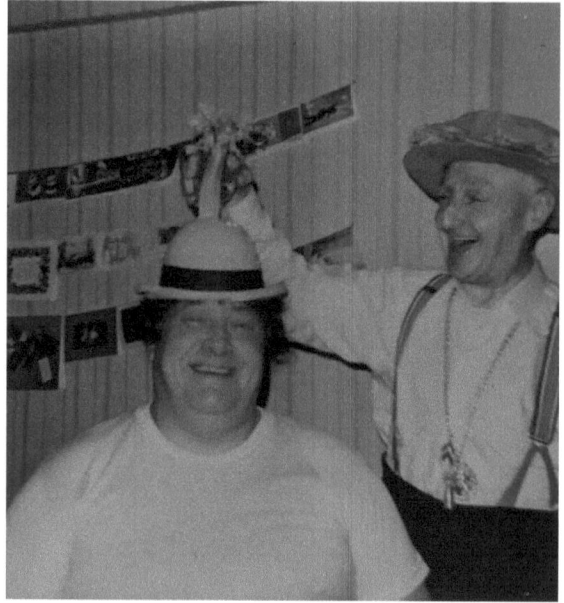

Dad and Uncle Jim early 1970s.

Living with my grandparents brought its problems. My Dad was very jealous and possessive and didn't like my Nan seeing me or making a fuss of me. We eventually moved to 17 Teesdale Street, London E2. It must have been very difficult for my Mum

Cordova Road, E3 with the factory in the background where the aunts begged for leftover lunch.

A same style house as I lived in Teesdale Street E2 but a bit posher.

who was a really easy-going person and was kind to everyone.

17 Teesdale Street was a three-storey house with a different family on each floor, we were on the top. Two bedrooms and a living room and kitchen combined. There was a toilet on the middle floor and an outside toilet in the yard. Bath night was every Friday in a tin bath in the living room and I was third in. Youngest always in last. During the week we had what was called a "cat's lick" which entailed washing with soap, water and a flannel in the kitchen sink. There were no locks on any of the doors to the flats. Nobody had anything worth stealing.

On 17 June 1950 my brother Harry was born.

Life in the East End was very simple. There weren't many cars on the roads, in fact I don't think anyone in our street had one, so playing out was safe. We could walk to the local parks to play. Next to Bethnal

Green Tube Station was a small park, which we called Barmy Park (named locally as there had been an 'institution' next to it) which had a library and a paddling pool. There was also a little fountain at the entrance into which my brother fell, complete in his new cowboy outfit, Mum was not very pleased. Victoria Park was further away so you would have to be taken by a parent.

I had quite a good childhood living in Teesdale Street. Children played in the streets, dressing up (especially if you had been a bridesmaid and had a fancy dress to wear) and putting on shows. I loved my roller skates. There was a little street, (ours was cobbled) between ours and the next street, Blythe Street, where the road was like glass, except for the odd pothole, and perfect for skating. Saturday morning pictures were a must for all kids. Can you imagine a whole cinema filled with just children?

There was a post recently on Facebook written by someone that lived a few streets from where I grew up that summed up life living in the East End in the 1950s.

"I grew up during a time when everyone treated each other like family, you could leave your front door open, and everyone that came to your house was your aunty or uncle even if they were no relation. We went outside to play on the streets, built dens and jumped in puddles to get mud off our shoes. We had to be home when the street lights came on as we didn't have mobiles. We got dirty climbing trees. We ate homemade food and chips were cooked in a chip pan. We got ice cream from the ice cream man if Mum was flush. We used to play Wars over the old Bomb Sites and a lump of dried mud/earth used to explode like a grenade. We played Tin Tan Tommy, Hide and Seek and even kiss chase. If we had a bottled drink we shared the same bottle after giving it a wipe with our mucky sleeves. We rode our bikes (in my case a three-wheeler) with no helmet and if we fell off we'd get gravel rash. If someone had a fight that's what it was, a fist fight – no guns or knives and your big brother or sister dealt with the bullies. The street lights were your curfew or until someone got hurt and school was mandatory. We watched our mouths around our elders because we knew we'd get a clip around the ear."

I was quite an extrovert when I was young and I

Me and a friend on our three wheeled bikes, Cordova Road, E3.

have been told that at the age of two I could be heard jumping around in my cot singing "Enjoy Yourself It's Later Than You Think".

When I was about three I remember my Dad shouting and my Mum crying. it didn't take him long to reveal his true character.

From the age of four, I went to the local school, Teesdale Street, (now apartments) which was at the other end of our street. Nursery, infants and then juniors. The teacher I had from the age of seven to 11 was Mrs George. She stood no nonsense and got 11 girls out of a class of 32 into grammar school. One of her teaching methods was to place a large clock (without the hands) on the blackboard and, with a ruler in each hand, point to two numbers on the clock, eg, 9 x 8. She would then say a name and you had to answer immediately. (The answer is 72 by the way.) Woe betide you if you didn't know your tables. Mrs George and I stayed friends until she died in 2005. She even crocheted Daniel a shawl when he was born.

I can remember the nurse coming to the junior school to see if anybody had head lice. We used to call her Nitty Nora.

Teesdale Street nursery c.1953.

Coronation Day 1953
Harry and me in "that" dress.

Me aged about 4 in Old Bethnal Green Road. The dress was green and white and my Dad got it from the American Embassy where he worked at the time.

Pearl and Wayne's wedding day 4 February 1956. They left to live in America two days later. See Nana's story.

For the Queen's Coronation in 1953 Mum had bought me this beautiful white organza dress trimmed with navy blue velvet and navy blue velvet spots on it. I was only allowed to wear it on Sundays (or as we would call it "high days and holidays".) When I grew out of it Mum gave it to the lady next door for her daughter (there were five children living in three rooms). She must have worn it continually for a week and as a result it was filthy. As we passed her one day I said to my Mum, in a not too quiet voice, "That dress never looked like that when I had it".

My Aunt Pearl got married in 1956 and the reception was held at Bethnal Green Town Hall. For the reception they had hired a live band and I drove the band mad to get up on stage to sing but my Mum kept telling them not to let me. After the interval and as the band started to play again, there I was, up on stage, preparing to sing the old Doris Day number "Secret Love". The audience loved it.

Growing up in the East End if you didn't like pie and mash with liquor there was something wrong with you. During the school holidays it was a treat to go to Kelly's pie and mash shop but because we didn't have a lot of money (I think one of the reasons for that was that my Dad was an unsuccessful gambler. They say you never find a poor bookmaker and Mum used to say that we'd have "If Only" put on his headstone) so could only afford mash and liquor.

Even now pie and mash is the thing I yearn for when I come back from a holiday abroad.

As we only had two bedrooms in Teesdale Street, my brother and I shared a room and I was getting to the age where I needed the privacy of my own room. My Dad was constantly up the Town Hall harassing

Kelly's pie and mash shop
Bethnal Green Road, E2 with the delicious pie and mash.
Unfortunately the shop has since closed down.

111 Bishops Way, E2 (on the right).

the housing office to let us have a bigger place. As she wasn't very accommodating he asked her if she had won her job in a lottery.

In 1957, we moved to a four storey Victorian house at 111 Bishops Way, E2. This time we had the top two floors with our own front door that locked, but the house was freezing. The only heat was from an open fire in the front room and although you were lovely and warm on your front, your back was cold. The room was also extremely large with two floor to ceiling windows. On the upside we had our own bathroom.

We only stayed there for two years and then moved to a brand new maisonette, 18 Bradley House E2, a newly built maisonette in a block of 54 flats. No sharing this time. I was 11 years old.

One day when I came home from work, my Mum opened the door for me and said "Whatever you do don't laugh". Well, as soon as someone says that you want to laugh. I walked into the kitchen and there was my Dad, laying on his back trying to undo the U bend of the sink. Apparently earlier he had broken two teeth off of his set of false teeth and put them in a cup of water by the sink to see if the dentist could reattach

Back of Bradley House, E2 c.1962.

them. Unfortunately, he forgot what he had done earlier and tipped the water and teeth down the sink. As soon as he told me what he was doing I burst into fits of laughter and got sent to bed. I was 24 years old and, of course, I went.

At the age of 11, I passed an entrance exam and got into Coborn Grammar School for Girls. Funnily enough it was the same school that my Aunt Pearl had attended. This was further away from where I lived so I had to get the underground. I used to meet my friend Pat and on the way from Mile End Station to school we would harmonise the Everly Brothers' song *Cathy's Clown*.

I wasn't that interested in school, probably too much distraction with football, but I loved playing netball, swimming and hockey. I did belong to a church youth club with some of the girls I went to school with that met once a week, although we never went to church. Don't know how that worked.

In the early 1960s, a film called *A Place To Go*, starring Mike Sarne, was being shot outside our flat, with the main character walking down Mansford Street and past our flat. My Dad was on the balcony

watching what was going on when a member of the production team asked if he would mind going inside. He replied saying when they paid his rent they could ask him to move. You can see him on the balcony in the film.

Around 1963 Spurs Supporters Club obtained the lease of a house next to the football club and was able to expand. They had a bar and lounge on one side downstairs and a shop on the other. Upstairs were like offices where you could book to go to away matches and dances. My whole family would attend the dance and, as many of the supporters lived in the East End, a coach would transport us. During the 1960s many of the players attended the dances and they were much more approachable than nowadays. This is where most of my teenage years were spent. Plus, there were Saturday match days and usually European football during the week. This was my life then.

I left school at the age of 17 having stayed on to do a commercial course (shorthand and typing). I hated it. I had taken my GCE's at 16 but only passed Maths. I did eventually retake my English GCE in 1983 and achieved an A*.

A still from the 1960s film A Place To Go with my Dad on the balcony.

My 21st birthday party, January 1969. The photo on the left is me cutting the cake and the photo on the right shows L-R Uncle Jim, Aunt Doll, Aunt Mable, nanny Lee, Queenie (the lady who crocheted Daniel's Christening gown), Aunt Mag and Aunt Charlotte.

Although a few of my friends went to the pub on weekends I never actually went in a pub until I was nineteen years old. Call me old fashioned but I thought it was wrong unless escorted by a gentleman friend. I soon made up for it though.

Sometimes, in my twenties, if I was going out and had to get a bus and didn't want to wear my specs my Mum would walk me to the bus stop to put me on the right bus.

My usual drinking hole was a pub called The Queens in Hackney Road. Sadly no longer there. Or a well-known pub in Bethnal Green called the Green Gate. Peters and Lee (Google them) sang there quite frequently. It was there I met my dear friend Pam. She had worked in the same office as a school friend called Christine who invited her to join us one Friday night. Pam unfortunately cut her foot on a broken glass and I ended up taking her to Bethnal Green A&E to have it seen to. She had to have a tetanus injection in her backside and a stitch in her foot. That started our friendship and now 57 years later (could be 58 by the time I've finished this book) we are still besties.

I had a great 21st birthday party held in a hall along by the Supporters Club. We had a live band, The Jet Set, and I wore a beautiful Grecian style dress which I still have but don't fit into. After the hall closed we carried on into the early hours in the Supporters Club.

In my early twenties I went out with a chap who worked in a jeweller next to Chancery Lane station, near to where I worked. We went to a pub and he bought a round of drinks. When asked if I wanted another he said he was a little short of money and could I pay. I gave him some money and he brought back the drinks and put them and my change on the table. I didn't like to pick it up. For the third drink he went to the bar after picking up my change that was laying on the table. When it was time to leave he asked if he could see me again. I replied saying I couldn't afford it.

My Dad used to say that he didn't need anybody. Karma is a strange thing. In 1973, after many years of verbal abuse, Mum decided to leave him and, as I was still living at home, I went with her. Mum and I talked about her leaving my Dad and she said she stayed because of us kids. For me she could have done it years earlier but I suppose it's embarrassing to make that kind of statement. Many's the time, if he was upset, he would say that my Nan and Grandad couldn't come for Christmas or that Mum couldn't go to the football. Her reply to not going to the football was when he paid for her to go then he could tell her

what to do. It wasn't the done thing in those days (you just put up and shut up) and women were mostly dependent on their husbands. In January 1971 my brother had married Sue and was living in Newbury Park and Mum had a good job, as did I, so she decided enough was enough. My brother moved to Spain in 2005, he hadn't spoken to my Mum for years and I haven't seen or spoken to him since then.

Over time, we would fill suitcases of belongings and take them to my Nan's as that's where we were going to live. On the day we left Mum wrote a note, leaving it on the mat so he would see it when he got home from work. In 1977, I got a call from the police to say that my Dad had been found dead and had been dead for about two weeks. Karma. When Mum and my brother went to the flat to sort things out they found the leaving note on top of the fridge in the kitchen.

Neither Mum nor Dad was tactile, probably due to their upbringing and while Mum was around it didn't seem to matter, she showed her love in many other ways, but it's something that has bothered me later in life. Plus, I was never told I was pretty and it was only when some 59ers (girls I met at my senior school in 1959) met for lunch and brought with them some past

Me, May 1968. That is all my own hair.

photos that it cropped up. When I was twenty, I went to a wedding of my school friend Glenis. She had sorted out some of her wedding photos to bring and came across one of me with our late friend Gill. It was only when her husband commented on how pretty I was that I realised I wasn't that bad looking. I think if I had been told when I was younger it would have given me more self-worth. ♠

MY NEAREST AND DEAREST

MY NAN AND GRANDAD LEE had a great influence on me. In my early years, most Sunday tea times and Christmases were spent at their house, unless we were otherwise occupied watching Spurs play at White Hart Lane. It was a happy and comfortable house even though there weren't the home comforts we have today. There was no heating in the house so most of the time was spent round the fire in the back of the house. It didn't take long for jelly in a mould to set in the front room, I can tell you. When my Nan got a telephone she would have to book a call to talk to her daughter Pearl (my aunt) in America.

Nan and Grandad Lee's wedding 25/12/1924. Second to the left of the groom is Aunt Doll Rose. Second to the right of the bride is Uncle Jim Rose. Two to the right of him is Aunt Mag and seated in front of her is my great grandmother, Charlotte.

Later on nan, Grandad and aunt Mag would spend Christmas with us in Bradley House. I've been trying to remember where everyone used to sleep, especially if Aunt Doll and Uncle Jim used to come as well. I remember one Christmas that they spent with us and I was getting ready to go out. I was all dressed up, with my makeup which included my blue eyeshadow. when my Grandad looked at me and said I looked like our blue budgerigar, Billy. I got my own back though. After an evening spent at the pub Christmas Eve, I came back home and everyone was in bed and as I went into the bathroom I spied seven pots with false teeth in them so what normal person who'd had a few drinks wouldn't swap them all around. You should've heard them the next morning trying to get "their" teeth in.

Nan was born in 1904 and was the youngest of seven children, although one died very young, and they were all very close and as children all lived in Cordova Road. At the bottom of the road was a factory and, because they were so poor, they used to stand outside and ask if they could have any unfinished

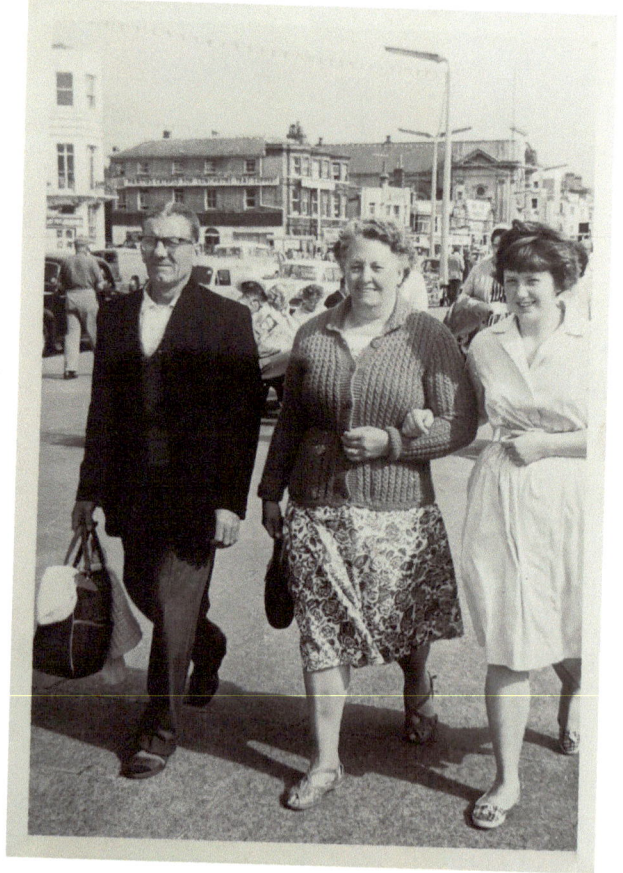

Nan, Grandad and me Great Yarmouth promenade c.1962.

Site of the destruction of the first flying bomb that killed my Grandad's sister Alice.

Aunt Mag and Aunt Charlotte wearing their Gert and Daisy rosettes. So named after two sisters called Elsie and Doris Walters who performed under those names. Incidentally they were both born in Bromley-by-Bow and went to Coborn School, as did I.

lunch from the workers. Nan mostly worked in clothing factories or laundries as a Hoffman presser, which was a very large machine for pressing clothes. All well and good in the winter but extremely uncomfortable in the summer.

My Grandad, born in 1903, liked a drink after work on a Friday night but never to excess, unless he was led astray. This never bothered my Nan unless it was Christmas Eve and they were coming to us and she would "clean" him. See explanations of sayings in another paragraph.

Most of his life he had been a lorry driver and being born in 1903 was too young to enlist in the First World War and his job made him necessary for the war effort during the Second World War. He had

Aunt Mag and Aunt Charlotte holding the FA Cup probably 1962.

never had proper schooling so couldn't read or write but knew roads like the back of his hand so that when road signs were dismantled, to confuse the Germans if they landed, he still knew where he was going.

Grandad liked to smoke, Woodbines being his choice of cigarette but it would be his downfall as he died in 1973 of lung cancer. Pearl came over from America for the funeral and as my Nan didn't have a suitable coat for the funeral we all went on a Number 8 bus to Oxford Street. Well, that was the intention, but the IRA had carried out a car bombing on the Old Bailey so never made it.

Grandad was the second eldest of three brothers and one sister but on recently checking facts on the Ancestry family tree it seems he had a half-brother as well. I remember the brothers and their families as we used to meet up regularly and I played with my cousins but never met his sister, Aunt Alice, as she was killed by the first flying bomb to fall on London – on 13 June 1944. There is a plaque on the side of the railway bridge denoting the event. After this, my Grandad kept a can of petrol in the backyard to do his worst if a German landed there.

Two of my Nan's sisters, Aunt Charlotte and Aunt

— say "**GERT AND DAISY**." Pictured in happy mood are our two zealous travelling sisters, Mrs. Patten and Mrs. Fuller—known to all supporters as "Gert and Daisy." Regular "Away" followers of Spurs for many more years than they care to remember, illness alone keeps them off the coach.

A picture from an article on Pinterest showing Aunt Mag and Aunt Charlotte with the Spurs' mascot, a cockerel.

Mag had lived together in Edmonton since 1936. Aunt Charlotte had a daughter Pat but unfortunately Aunt Mag couldn't have children so spent a lot of her time with Grace and Jim. They were also football mad and I am told that Aunt Mag went to the 1921 Cup Final.

Aunt Mag was the Bank of England in our family. She won a High Court case against the army and was awarded a war widow's pension for the death of her husband Tom. Although he died a few years after returning from India in the First World War he had picked up an infection while serving there. She could afford the mortgage of a house. She would be the one to go to if you wanted to borrow money. As she got older Aunt Mag's memory started to wane and on one occasion, when being repaid a debt, she'd forgotten she had lent any money. That's when we knew. And she would repeat herself quite a lot. I wouldn't mind a £1 for every time she told us that as children they used to sleep in a bed, three at the top and three at the bottom. She would constantly ask the same question over and over and we would reply "Yes, Aunt Mag". I notice that my children say this to me now.

Other than away matches, the two aunts travelled to all the European Cup matches during the 1960s. One time there was an article about them in the local paper and on their next trip abroad their house was burgled.

Aunt Mag came out with some wonderful phrases, for instance if you were driving too fast she would say "You're doing the knots". And when they were little she would call Daniel, my son, "little bits" and Sally, my daughter, "slapcabbage".

During the war my Nan, Grandad, Mum and Pearl moved from the East End to Edmonton because the docks were getting bombed regularly. They had an air raid shelter at the bottom of the garden and when the sirens went off they would all sleep down there. The adults would take it in turns to put out the candle which was done by wetting two fingers and squeezing

A young Aunt Mag and Tom Fuller (Aunt Mag's husband) c.1910.

the flame. Not Aunt Mag, she would blow it out and everyone would moan at her because the candle smelled foul.

At the beginning of the war my Mum was evacuated to the country. She wasn't there long as on a visit from my Nan my Mum was found to have nits. Nan brought her home immediately.

On a trip to America on the Queen Mary to my Aunt Pearl, my Nan, Grandad and Aunt Mag were having dinner and the waiter asked Aunt Mag if she wanted her coffee black or white. She asked for black but when he brought her the black coffee she asked him where the milk was. You can take the girl out of the East End but you can't take the East End out of the girl.

My Nan also had two brothers, one of which died when he was very young. The other one, Uncle Tom, loved animals. Many's the time he brought home stray dogs and when he married and lived in Shotgate, Wickford he reared greyhounds. They used to live in their own little house and had bunk beds and if any of them got sick he used to sleep with them. Uncle Tom couldn't get on with false teeth but could easily eat an apple with his gums.

Aunt Mag used to torment him singing "Thomas Josiah piddled in the fire". ♠

COCKNEY IDIOMS

OVER THE YEARS I have picked up many of the sayings from the elders in the family and sometimes I would come out with them and Sally and Daniel would look at me inquisitively. Here are a few.

Sod all, Henry Hall's brother.

Mucking fuddle (change the first letters of each word around – self-explanatory).

When someone had been divorced or similar and you asked them if they would get married again they would come out with the phrase **"I wouldn't have another man if his arse hung in diamonds."**

If you were having an argument with someone you would say **"I'm going to knock your eye out and spit in the hole"**. Not very pleasant I know. Jokingly my Nan once said this to Alan, my husband at that time, forgetting that he had a false eye.

On the rob. Stealing.

As mentioned previously about my Nan cleaning my Grandad after having too much to drink, it means really having a go at them.

Shanks' pony - a mode of transport - your feet

Men and boys are renowned for not being able to find what they are looking for, even if it's right under their nose. I remember my Grandad calling out to my Nan when he was looking for something and her calling back **"It's up the old woman's arse next door"**.

A couple of times I have said things to Catherine and Sally has looked at me quizzically. One being that if she is getting her ready to go out I would say **"Are you going tats?"** and the second is if she was tired I would ask her if she was peepies. Both phrases used when I was growing up. ♠

![acorn ornament]

THE SUBURBS

UP UNTIL WE BOUGHT A HOUSE in Ilford in 1975 every place I had lived had been rented from the council.

Around November 1973 I met Alan at a small gathering organised by a neighbour and on the 28 December 1974 we got married at Hackney Town Hall Registry Office. We moved into a small flat at 7b Belsham Street, Hackney, E9. It was a double fronted house split into 4 flats. Once again with an outside toilet. We stayed there for nine months and then bought a three bedroom house at 76 De Vere Gardens, Ilford, Essex. It cost £11,200, having got an £11,000 mortgage from Hackney Council. Alan did a lot of work to the house and both Daniel

My wedding day 28 December 1974. L-R Alan's Uncle George Gibson, Sue (a girl I worked with), Mum, me, Alan, Alan's Mum Sophia and his stepfather Frank Herbert.

76 De Vere Gardens, Ilford, bottom right flat.

7 Belsham Street E9.

and Sally were born at King George's Hospital, (now apartments) while we lived there. We sold the house for approximately £36,000.

In 1976 Cordova Road was being demolished by the council to make way for a new park area and the residents had to move out. After looking at several properties Mum plumped for 48 Wyemead Crescent, Chingford. It was a fairly new build, and compared to Cordova Road had all mod cons. Unfortunately my Nan never lived to enjoy it for very long as she died of ovarian cancer in February 1977.

Until I had Daniel on 17 December 1978, I still went to football matches. When Daniel was due I remember my contractions starting early in the evening but wouldn't go to the hospital until I had watched Match Of The Day. I don't know what all the fuss was about as he never arrived until 9.30 the next morning. Sally was born on the 25 November 1981 at 8.30am and was 12 days late. I remember going to the football on the 21 November but being eight days

overdue I couldn't get through the turnstiles so had to go to a nearby big gate manned by a policeman. I mentioned I couldn't get through the turnstiles as I was pregnant and he kindly asked me when I was due. As he opened the gate I told him "Eight days ago" and he couldn't usher me in quick enough to get away from me.

In 1979 Aunt Mag went to live with my Mum. Aunt Charlotte had become poorly and went to live with her daughter, Pat. Aunt Mag was a bit deaf so didn't often join in conversations and was prone to repeating herself. At times Aunt Mag could be quite trying especially when it came to hearing aids. When Mum went off to work she would put the hearing aid in for Aunt Mag and turn it on but during the day Aunt Mag would take it out and put it in her apron. Unfortunately, she didn't turn it off and it would aggravate Honey, the dog, who would bite at the apron and break it. Mum gave up after two broken hearing aids.

About 1981 Mum did a house swap for a property

Aunt Mag early 1980s.

in Winslow Grove which she eventually bought.

In December, 1982 we moved to 8 Crescent Road, Chingford, E4 a really beautiful 5 bedroom Victorian house and once again Alan did a lot of work on it but he was rather slow. It cost approximately £90,000. The only room he ever completed without stopping was the basement in which he had a full-size snooker table. It took two years for the kitchen to be usable and only when we were selling did all the knobs get put on the kitchen units.

When Daniel started school in Easter 1983 I started chatting to some of the other Mums at the school gates and it was there that I met Beryl, Bet and Joy and a wonderful friendship began.

Life meandered along during the 1980s and 1990s with Daniel and Sally taking up most of my time. But as they got a little older I was able to get back to going to football and I would go to work at our factory. We made reproduction furniture. One good thing to come out of working in the factory was the sawdust under my fingernails stopped me biting my nails. Sometimes my Mum would come and help and Aunt Mag would sit in a chair and watch. One day, as we were leaving, Aunt Mag said she couldn't leave as she was waiting for Charlotte. When Mum informed her that Charlotte had died she replied saying nobody had told her. That memory again.

During some of the holidays my friend Pam and her children Daniel and Belinda would come and stay and we had the perfect arrangement. She didn't like cooking that much and I hated going out when the weather got above 68 degrees so she would take all the kids over to the forest and I would stay indoors cooking – with the curtains closed to keep out the heat of the day.

On one occasion we started to bathe Sally and Belinda and Belinda was covered in spots, Chicken Pox, which both my kids then got.

Bedtime was a nightmare with them all, up and down. I used to shout at them "Get up them stairs, and get up them stairs NOW" and they still tease me on my cockney accent.

As Daniel and Sally got older I was able to blood them to the game and the team, of course.

On my fortieth birthday Alan arranged a surprise party at a pub (organised totally by my Mum and me)

and I got the opportunity to sing on the stage. Again.

Shortly after Aunt Mag died in 1988, Mum moved to Great Yarmouth and Sally would spend most of the holidays with her. Mum would still travel by coach back to Chingford for football, though. On one occasion she walked all the way from her house to the bus station with her skirt inadvertently tucked in her knickers. Luckily, some kind person at the bus station told her about it.

8 Crescent Road, E4 with Daniel sitting on the steps and me in our front room (with good old William Shakespeare).

Beryl, Angie, Bet, me, Monica and Joy at Beryl's daughter's wedding 1991.

In 1994 I entered a competition with the Daily Mirror and as you can see I won, the prize being a crate of Carling Lager. I don't drink beer but Alan was happy.

Around 1995/96 life at home wasn't a happy time. Alan wasn't very interested in going to work and I was working full time and running the house, cooking, cleaning etc. We had planned to sell the house and

Cutting from the Daily Mirror.

move to Norfolk but I never really warmed to the idea as I didn't think things would improve so around May 1996 I decided around that, when contracts were exchanged on the house, I was going to tell Alan I wanted out of the marriage.

The house was sold on the 19 July 1996 and for three months Daniel, Sally and I lived in a flat above jewellers in Station Road, Chingford. I bought 7 Hoppett Road, Chingford, E4 on 1 November 1996 for £78,000 and this is currently where I live.

Everywhere I have lived I have been blessed with good neighbours. In Ilford my next door neighbour was a lady called Monica. Every day she would walk into town to do some shopping and when Daniel came along she would regularly take him in his pram and in return I would do some washing for her as she didn't have a machine. Her daughter Janet would love looking after Daniel and would babysit so that I could go to the football.

When I moved to 8 Crescent Road there was a lovely couple and their daughter who lived at 9a. Jill, John (who happened to be a Spurs fan too) and Holly. As I didn't have Sky at the time he would often invite me to watch sport at his house, especially when the Ryder Cup was on.

Sally and me at my fiftieth birthday lunch.

Home, Sweet Home, Chingford, E4.

My fiftieth birthday lunch. Left Elaine Watkins, me and Daniel, pulling one of his faces.

On the day I moved I was in a terrible state, still packing and Jill called in and saw me crying so enlisted the help of another neighbour, Jane, to help me.

Now I'm in Hoppett Road it's like Ramsay Street (without the affairs) and we all look out for each other.

Life settled into a nice routine during this time. Daniel went off to University at the LSE and although

he was still based in London, he lived in Halls and often on a Saturday or Sunday I would have six hungry students sitting at my kitchen table eating either beef or chicken stew. I loved it.

For my fiftieth birthday I hired out a restaurant in Station Road and my Mum bought me a Mr Blobby birthday cake. I loved Mr Blobby.

During my fifties I often frequented the theatre, musicals were my favourite, with my theatre buddy, Dave.

Sally was attending Woodford County High School

and was studying for her A Levels. In 1999 she went off to study at King's College, also in London, and stayed in Halls. Do you think it was something I'd done?!?

Dave, my theatre buddy. Also a lifelong Spurs fan. Looks like a photo bomb.

Mum's eightieth birthday party.

Mum always loved Great Yarmouth, having spent most of her holidays there as a child. Unfortunately she had bouts of being unwell and being so far away I persuaded her to move back. On 1 November 2000 she came to live with me.

Often, if a football match on Sky Sports clashed with motor racing that was on BBC, we'd take the portable television into the front room so we could watch both at the same time. We'd watch everything: Football, motor racing, athletics, rugby union, swimming, tennis and cricket.

In 2005 we found out that the pains Mum had been suffering were caused by a bladder stone. During the operation to remove the stone they found some cancerous cells in her bladder and every three months she would go for an exploratory operation called a cystoscopy (she'd call it an up periscope). She would eventually succumb to the horrible disease on 12 October 2011. Four days after she died I had recorded highlights of an Indy Car Race as it was on too late to watch live. When I went to watch the recorded highlights the next day they had been cancelled as there had been a fatal accident and the British driver Dan Weldon had been killed. I turned to tell my Mum and she wasn't there.

The manner of Mum dying has been a thorn in my side, and, despite many efforts to get the hospital to acknowledge their mistakes, this will never be resolved. Even our local Member of Parliament, Iain Duncan Smith took an interest and agreed with my finding but to no avail. It's quite unbelievable that where money is involved you get six years grace to sort things out. With a life it's one year. ♠

MY CHILDREN

NO STORY would be complete without some stories about Daniel and Sally. It's a mother's duty to embarrass their children.

When Daniel was about three we went on our usual pilgrimage to Great Yarmouth and Mum took him to see Punch and Judy on the beach. I actually think it was more for her than him but having a child with you makes it more legit. He was sitting near the front when Policeman Jack told the audience to be aware that the alligator was crawling under the sand and that it might bite. He was the only child to get up and run.

At about four he watched a Tom and Jerry cartoon where one of the characters was playing the piano. He immediately asked if he could learn the piano. I had read somewhere that you should always encourage children if they wanted to learn so took him to piano lessons. He couldn't even read so I'm still unsure how he learnt.

Also at the age of four years and four months Daniel started school at Normanhurst, a private school. Up until then he hadn't been interested in reading or writing but by the July that all changed. I remember his teacher, Mrs Collin, saying that Daniel didn't much like writing but he loved maths so that when she wanted him to write a story she would suggest he write 40 words. On one occasion

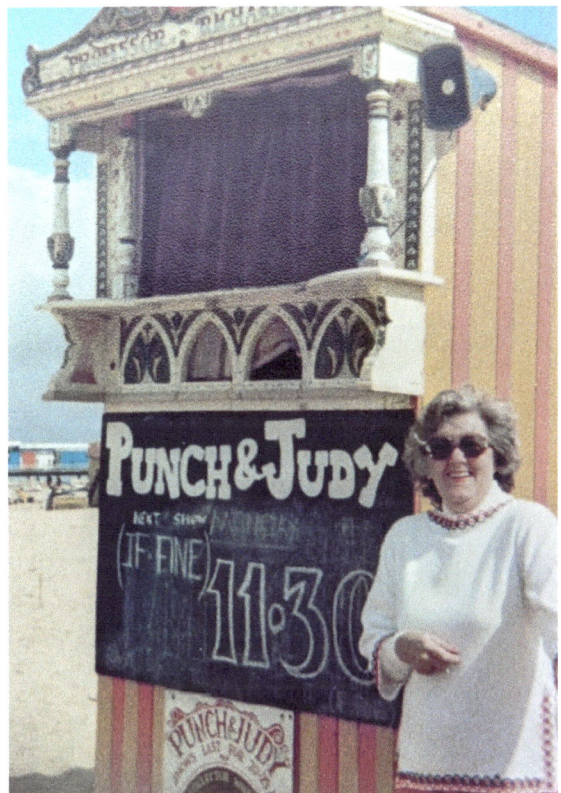

Mum on Great Yarmouth beach.

the topic was a snowman and when he had got to about 35 words he ended it by saying "the sun came out and it melted". It was also Mrs Collin who suggested I do something better schoolwise for Daniel. I hadn't realised he was gifted.

Daniel went to Forest School at the age of six on a

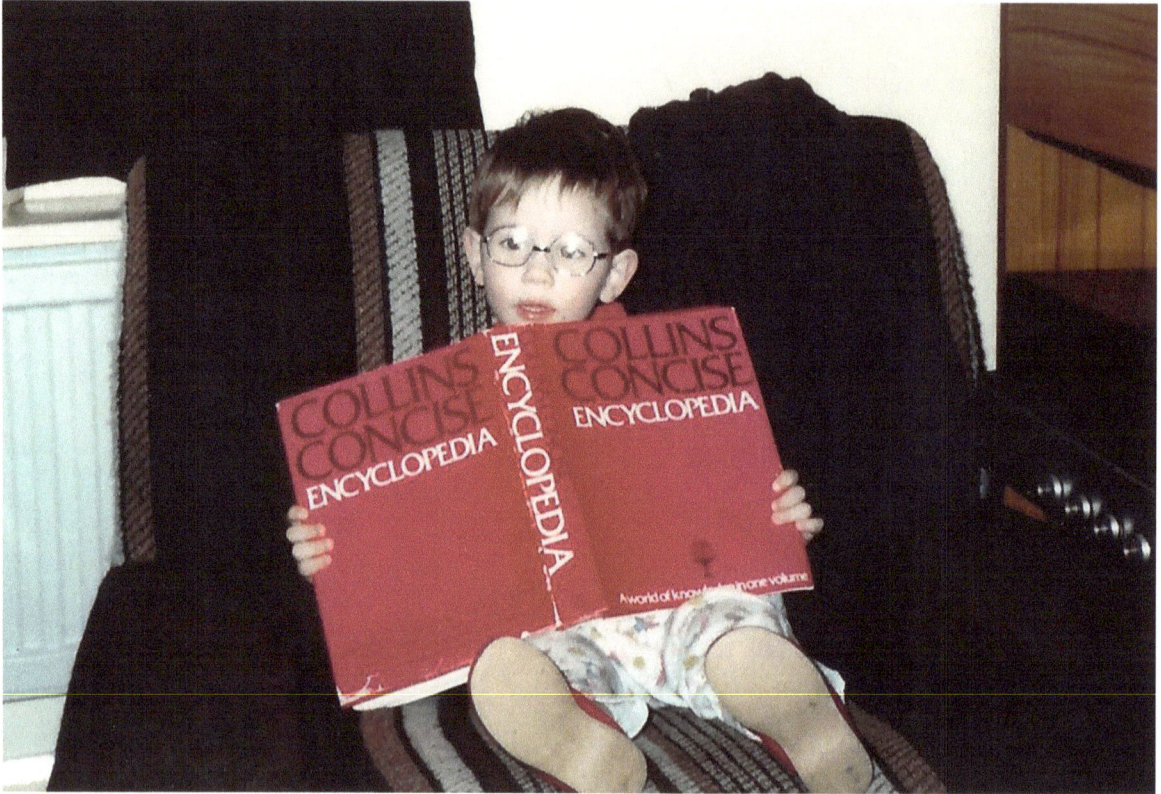

Daniel – early learning.

Daniel's Graduation day with me, Nan Honor, Daniel and Alan. Nan looking like she's bombed the photo.

Sally, Covent Garden day trip c.1985.

Sally in class with Mrs. Miller and the local MP Steven Norris.

Sally and Mark's wedding day 20 July 2013.

Sally and me.

Sally and Daniel.

Daniel and Laura.

one-third Scholarship where he learnt the phrase "Hip Hip Hooray". He thought it was "tip it away" so that's what he would shout.

At about seven Mum and I would sometimes take him to the football although he wasn't very interested in the game then, he'd rather read a comic. At the time there was a miner's strike and the crowd were shouting out rude comments about Arthur Scargill. When we got home he said to his Dad that he didn't know Scargill was a (I held my breath) banker.

After being at Forest School for a few terms Daniel saw there was money to be earned by getting me to take him to buy jars of sweets, eg. Cola Bottles, from Makro, putting them into bags and selling them for a small profit but undercutting the school tuck shop.

One Christmas spent with my Mum at Great Yarmouth, Daniel happened to get the rubber end of a

pencil stuck in his ear. I had to take him to the local hospital to get it removed by a doctor who told him to never put anything smaller than his elbow in his ear.

Daniel was always a year above his age so that at 14 he passed his Maths GCSE and at 15 he got another nine.

My last funny story was at his graduation. Dressed in his robe, he walked up the steps, across the stage to collect his certificate and down the steps on the other side. Only he didn't make it as the sleeve of his robe got caught on the rail and dragged him back. There was a lot of laughter in the hall.

Sally had a totally different character to her brother. She was very shy and it was a great surprise to me when she wanted to do dancing. Even more so when she appeared in a show at Walthamstow as a Care Bear.

All through her school life Sally was the peacemaker, kids going to her to sort out their bullying

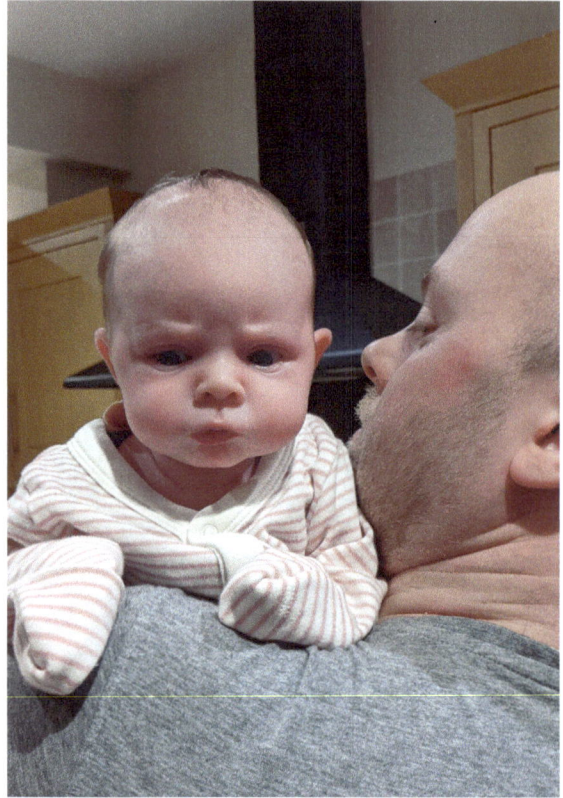

Granddaughter Catherine Grace.

problems. One time when she was about seven, a boy in her class was picking on another student and, as she just happened to have a pencil in her hand, stabbed him in the chest. Apparently it only slightly broke the skin! And he definitely deserved it. (Her words).

When she was about eight we went to Butlin's for a holiday. I had bought Sally a lovely red and white striped swimming costume but when she had a bath later her torso was covered in brown and white stripes. We laughed so much, she wasn't a happy bunny.

Between the ages of eight and eleven, Sally went to Coopersale Hall School and her first teacher was a former Mayor of Epping. Very proper, no nonsense, old schoolteacher. By this time Sally had found her feet in life and could be quite direct, although always fair. On first meeting Mrs Miller at a Parents' Evening I was quite taken aback to be told that Sally was the rudest child she had ever taught. But she must have turned out okay as over 30 years later they are still

friends. She even gave Sally money when she first went to university.

When Sally left university she continued her studies at the Institute of Education, training to be a teacher and has been a teacher at St. Aubyn's school ever since. Daniel worked for a Fund Management company but left to pursue his dream of developing an app called Loose Ends. He is also a director of a few companies.

When Sally first met her future husband Mark, and I hadn't, I made her show me where he lived just in case anything untoward happened and I could sort him out.

On the 20 July 2013 Sally married Mark Slade, with the ceremony taking place at St. Mary's Church, Chigwell. Sally refused to spend an exorbitant amount of money on her wedding, so they had the reception in the garden of Mark's house. They spent more money on the honeymoon in the British

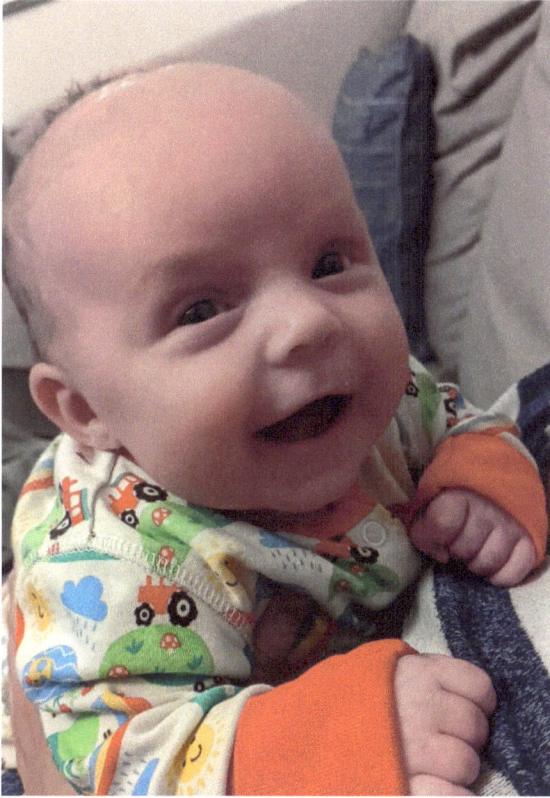

Virgin Islands, than the wedding! The day before the wedding we had a marquee erected in the garden and we set about putting up bunting and laying out the tables and chairs with the help of two cousins, Mark and Kelly, who had come over from America. Their parents, Karen (who is my first cousin and the daughter of Aunt Pearl) and her husband Vinny, were supposed to come as well but Karen wasn't able to fly. We had afternoon tea, a BBQ in the evening and a live singer.

It was at the wedding that I first met Laura, Daniel's girlfriend, who he had been seeing for 9 months. She is a travel writer for The Metro and so nice. She and Daniel have travelled the world together.

When Sally and Mark sold the house in Bourne Gardens, Chingford (he was part owner with his Dad, Ken) I offered to store Ken's boxes in my loft. I didn't realise he had 23. He has whittled down about 8 into one box but the other 15 are still up there. He had

electricity bills from the 1960s and some old DVDs of his Mum's.

Mark used to constantly torment me but not so much now as he wants to keep me on side for babysitting but I have to remind him every week to put the refuse bins out.

I cannot complete this section without mentioning my beautiful granddaughter, Catherine Grace. She has given me so much pleasure and it really pains me to think that arriving so late in my life I will not get to see her grow into womanhood. Before she came along I had never given much thought to the idea of being a Nan and would say you can't miss what you never had. I am so thankful that I felt this way as it would have been heart-breaking if I had known how it feels now and she had never come along. ♠

FOOTBALL, MY FIRST LOVE

FOOTBALL HAS PLAYED a big part in my life and there are so many anecdotes that I hope I can remember most of them.

When I was two my Mum couldn't get a babysitter for me so took me to the football with her. (You have to know that female babysitters were hard to find in our family as all the women and my Dad went to the football.) Anyway, she had a seat in the East Stand, front row. In those days children were allowed to sit on their parents laps and not have to pay. At some point during the game she looked over the stand and saw people below who were standing looking up. I was spitting on their heads.

Luckily, I grew out of that habit and from the age of 7 was a regular visitor to White Hart Lane with my Mum, Nan and two great aunts. My Nan and aunts also took me to all the away matches where we would travel by coach. I've been to so many towns and cities but only saw inside the football stadiums. Travelling by coach was fun and there was a lot of singing going on. In the 1950s Tottenham had a goalkeeper called Ted Ditchburn and every time an opposing forward would get near the goal Aunt Charlotte would shout out "Shut the gate Ted". He even told us later that sometimes he would hear her.

Most of our away coach trips and dances were organised through the Spurs Supporters Club. This was formed in 1948 and started life in a little kiosk to the side of the old main entrance to the ground. My Nan and Aunt Patsy were on the first committee. I believe they obtained the lease for Warmington House in 1963 and it became a popular meeting place for fans before and after the game.

When I was younger my family and I used to stand down the front, halfway line enclosure. This was an area just below the Directors Box. You paid a few more pennies to stand there but it was a smaller area than some of the other parts of the ground. The same crowd of people would be there every week. And because you were standing up you would mimic the movements of the players (it's the only way I can explain it) e.g., jump to head the ball, shoulder charge a player. When we graduated to having a season ticket in the Stand (seats) sometimes it would be hard to control yourself. At one game I shoulder charged my Mum and in turn she knocked a man off the end seat.

We used to have what we called a sweep (nowadays it's called a Sweepstake) and draw names of players out of a hat and the winner was the one who had the scorer of the first goal. A chap named Ray used to hold the winnings and one week he ran off with the money. We never saw him again.

One New Year's Eve, my friend John turned up at the game all dressed up, suit, pristine white shirt and

Inaugural Spurs Supporters Club Committee. Nanny Lee bottom left and Aunt Patsy, bottom right.

Halfway line enclosure White Hart Lane. In the photo, front row, are Aunt Mag, Nan, Pearl, Patsy, Dad and Aunt Charlotte.

This was taken when I was 2 or 3; I am the toddler being held by dad at the front of the image.

A decade later and still a fan: 13 year old me is third from the right. Taken in 1961, a good year for Spurs!

tie as he was going straight out to a do. The pitch in those days was more mud than grass and it being winter it was especially muddy. All of a sudden the ball was kicked and was headed our way. John thought he was being really clever and put his hand up to stop the ball, whereas the most sensible of us had ducked, but he hadn't reckoned on the momentum of the mud. He got covered in mud from his head and all the way down to his waist. His pristine white shirt was no longer pristine. Those around him were hysterical.

In the 1960/61 season Tottenham won the double, this was the League and the FA Cup, and had not been achieved since the 1896/97 season. I had been to nearly all the games for the league and when Spurs won the semi-final of the FA Cup a ballot was held for fans to win the opportunity to buy a Cup Final ticket. Unfortunately, I wasn't one of the lucky ones. But it just so happened that a lady working with my Mum at the time, had a boyfriend who knew quite a lot of the players and he took me to the White Hart pub that stood on the corner of the ground and main entrance. Bearing in mind I was only 13, but did look older.

My footballing idol of all was Bobby Smith and because I had been to many away games with my aunts and the Supporters Club held dances to which the players would come he recognised me. He asked if I had got a Cup Final ticket to which I replied I hadn't. He then said to get my Mum to take me to his house the following Sunday for tea and he would let me have a ticket. The following Sunday Mum and I had to take three buses to get from Bethnal Green to Palmers Green and he gave me a ticket and wouldn't even take payment. I was even shown his England caps. I don't think until then that there were actual caps. They were pale blue and felt like velvet.

Also in the early 1960s we went on a trip to Sheffield to see United play Spurs. At that time Sheffield shared their Bramall Lane ground with Yorkshire Cricket Club. The pitches were side by side and I was lucky enough to be on the football pitch side. You would

Bobby Smith and me Spurs Supporters Club dance 1960.

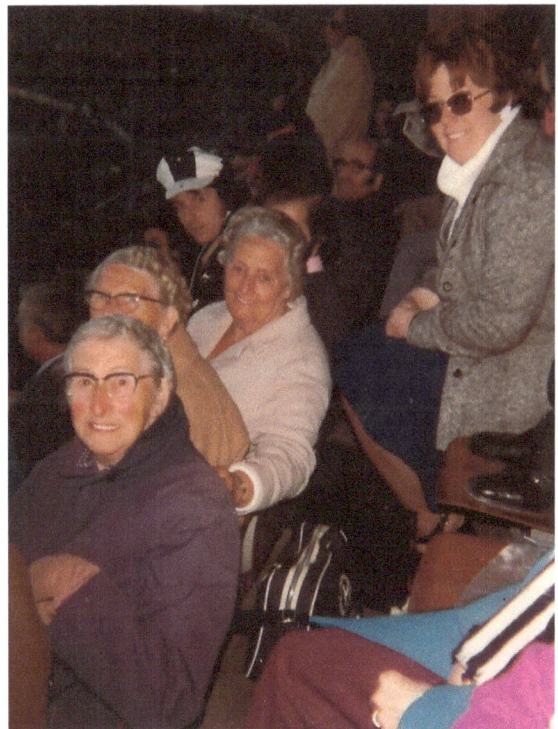

Aunt Charlotte, Aunt Mag, Nan and me European Cup Winners Cup May 1963. Mum was there but she was taking the photo.

Photo from the local newspaper, The Hackney Gazette, prior to Spurs beating Chelsea 2-1 in the Cup Final of 20 May 1967. I'm the "P".

have needed binoculars to see from the cricket side.

Due to Spurs winning the league they qualified for the European Cup (now known as the Champions League) but weren't successful, getting beat in the semi-final by Benfica. My two great aunts had gone to Portugal for the first leg and said Spurs were the victims of some terrible decisions by the referee who controversially disallowed two goals. I really thought we were in with a chance at the return leg and cried my eyes out on Aunt Charlotte's shoulder at the final whistle when we lost.

During an earlier round in that campaign we played a Polish side, Górnik Zabrze, and the Polish press described Spurs as "no angels" due to rough tackling. In the return leg some Spurs fans dressed up as angels and paraded around the pitch holding placards with slogans "Glory be to shining White Hart Lane" and "Rejoice! This is the night of vengeance". The crowd started singing "Glory, Glory Hallelujah" and a tradition was born. Spurs won the match 8-1.

Before a match my family and I would go to the Supporters Club and it was there that I met a couple of guys, Tony and Mick, who would turn out to be really good friends and a lot of fun. Sometimes before a game they would pick me up from Bradley House and we would drive to Saville Row where Tony would get measured for a suit. The tailor would bring out drinks and it was a whole different scene to what I was used to.

Spurs again won the FA Cup in 1962 and as a result qualified for the European Cup Winners' Cup (now called the Europa League) getting all the way to the final held in Rotterdam on the 15 May the following year. As I was still at school I had to play hookie to go. I had a biology teacher at that time called Miss Turvey, who happened to be a Wolves supporter, and we often discussed football. As I was due to have a lesson that day with her she commented to the class that my absence couldn't possibly have anything to do with football. If only she knew. We beat Atletico Madrid 5-1 and became the first British team to win a major European trophy. In 1972 Spurs won the inaugural UEFA Cup and again in 1984. Once again we got to a final played in Rotterdam in 1974 but got beat. There was a bit of crowd trouble (started by the police pulling down banners at half time) and we had to make a quick exit away from the ground.

The FA Cup final match against Chelsea in 1967 was the first occasion I had ever come across football hooliganism when Chelsea supporters threw a brick through the window of the Spurs Supporters Club coach that my Mum and Dad were travelling in.

During the 1960s and 1970s, I used to take some of my friends with me when I went to football matches and I remember on one occasion taking my friend Ann on a trip to Leeds. We had one of those trains where there were individual carriages off on a long corridor. There were about eight of us in this carriage, all fellow fans, plus Ann who was just along for the ride. At that time handmade boots were the rage and she had on a brand new pair of grey velvet boots. With the beer flowing around Ann spent the whole trip on the end seat with her legs outside the carriage.

After leaving Spurs Bobby Smith joined Brighton and Hove Albion and helped them become champions of the fourth division. For the last game of that 1964/65 season my Dad took me to Brighton and after the game we saw Bob and he gave me a big kiss on the cheek. At that time Norman Wisdom was their chairman and he was walking around as if he had had a few too many drinks.

Over the years, well after he had "hung up his boots", if he was at a function at White Hart Lane eg. a testimonial, he would take Mum and I into one of the lounges and buy us a drink.

Sadly on 18 September 2010 Daniel telephoned me to tell me that they had announced at Spurs that he had died. I have had a letter printed on the Sky Teletext page mentioning him. Through the club I found out where and when his funeral was being held and wrote his wife a condolence letter. I had to go. The funeral was held in Palmers Green and as I walked from the bus stop to the church I was approached by three people asking me if this was the right place for Bob's funeral. They were Peter Baker, his wife, and Sandra who had been the widow of John White, a former player. We chatted as we walked to the church and I told them the story of the Cup Final ticket. At the church Terry Dyson was one of the ushers (Cliff Jones was the other but he hadn't arrived yet) and was sorting out where people should sit (there were also representatives from Chelsea, a club Bob had played for before joining Spurs). When he asked who I was I once again told the story of the Cup Final ticket and he told me that he knew all about me.

In the church I was sitting next to two ladies who turned out to be the daughters of Cliff Jones and once again told them my story of the Cup Final ticket. After the ceremony there was to be a cremation service for close friends and family. As I walked to the bus stop a car pulled up beside and it was Cliff Jones' daughters who were going to give me a lift to the crematorium. I said I was going home but they insisted I went with them. At the crematorium I knew nobody and was wondering how I was going to get home when a lady approached me. She turned out to be Bob's stepdaughter and, of course, wondered who I was. Once again I repeated the story and she insisted I join them for the wake. She arranged for someone to take me and I ended up in one of the lounges at Tottenham among many of the players I grew up watching. Certainly a wow moment.

On my way home I texted Sally and told her I had just been to the best funeral ever. She texted back to say that the police had files on people like me and they ended in – path (psychopath and sociopath).

SPORTS LETTERS

I was so sad to read of the death of Spurs striker Bobby Smith. Most people thought of him as just a bustling old fashioned centre forward but I think his 13 goals in 15 games for England proved he was more than that. I met him on many occasions and he even gave me a 1961 Cup Final ticket and refused payment.

Yours sincerely,
Hazel Lewis

The letter printed on the Sky Teletext
Sunday 19th September 2010.

Since the sixties I have been to every Cup Final that Tottenham have played in except the Manchester City replay in 1981 after we had drawn the first game 1-1 after extra time. As it was a Wednesday evening game, and being three months pregnant with Sally, I was too tired to make the short trip again. I watched the replay on the television which we won 3-2. This game will be remembered by many, even non Spurs fans, for the remarkable Ricky Villa goal.

In 1985 I was lucky enough to go to see Spurs play at the Bernabéu, home of Real Madrid, although the atmosphere was a bit hostile and we were spat on by Madrid fans sitting nearby. We drew the match 0-0 but unfortunately we had lost the first leg 0-1 so were out of the competition. Before we left Madrid, we were able to visit the stadium and see their trophy room. More precious metal than in the Bank of England I suspect.

The highlight of my" footballing career" has to be going to the World Cup in 1966. The date, 30 July. My Mum and Dad had bought two blocks of ten tickets for all the games held at Wembley. I think they paid £5 each for them. Mum and Dad went to a few and I remember my Mum and Nan going to the Argentina game but have no idea why they didn't want to go to the final. I was going to take my friend John. A school friend called Carol (who was an Orient supporter) was also going with her friend Marshall and as he had a mini he offered to drive us all. I remember walking around the ground and John buying a flag and a replica Jules Rimet trophy but cannot recall any of the games except for John waving his flag so much the stitching came undone.

After the game we all went back to my flat in the East End where Mum had made us tea. As she opened the door John presented her with the replica trophy saying Bobby Moore had let him borrow it to show her but he needed to take it back. She also sewed his flag back together.

We decided to go up the West End that evening, carefully fixing the flag to the side of the car. We drove around Oxford Street (where somebody stole the flag off the car) and then on to Knightsbridge where the England team were having their celebratory dinner. I got chatted up by a Russian footballer and later, when we walked up Oxford Street at about 1am I noticed Eusebio, the world famous Portuguese footballer nicknamed The Black Pearl, walking towards me. As I scurried around in my bag looking for a pen and paper to get his autograph, he pulled out a photo of himself and signed it for me. Coincidentally Eusebio played for Benfica, who were the team to knock Tottenham out of the European Cup in 1962.

What a day. ♠

WE'RE ALL GOING ON A SUMMER HOLIDAY

GROWING UP if we went on holiday it would always be to Great Yarmouth. I loved the arcades and the donkey rides. One year I nagged my Nan so much for just one more ride that when she relented she told the donkey's keeper to go so fast it would put me off asking again.

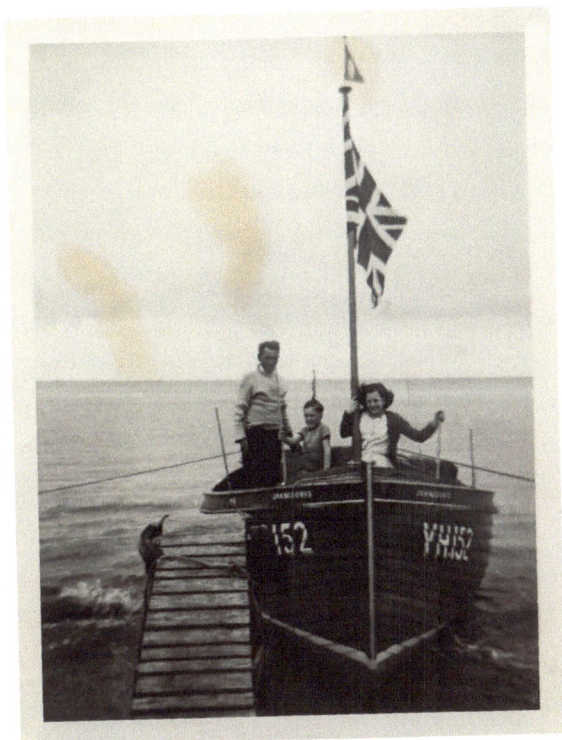

"Uncle" Ernie's boat, Great Yarmouth c. 1956.

You could also take a boat ride out to see the seals. I don't know how it happened but there was a skipper with a boat that we called Uncle Ernie. He wasn't an actual uncle but every day we would go out on his boat.

My first trip on an aeroplane was with Aunt Mag (I'm sure she paid) and Aunt Charlotte and we went to Jersey for the Battle of Flowers. This was an annual carnival with a parade of flower floats first staged in 1902.

At the age of 15 the family went on holiday with the Spurs Supporters Club to Cattolica, Italy and two years later I went on a two-centre holiday to Rome and Cattolica with my friend Avril. We flew into Rimini and then travelled by coach to Rome. On the coach were four other girls travelling in pairs and we all stayed together for the rest of the holiday. I stayed friends with Flo (real name Eileen) – one of the other pairs – for many years after. It still amazes me how my parents let me go away alone.

From then on I went to some wonderful places with girlfriends. Ibiza, a few times to Benidorm (I must add that they were more civilised in my day), Santa Ponsa, Majorca and Budva to name just a few. On one of the trips to Benidorm, this must have been

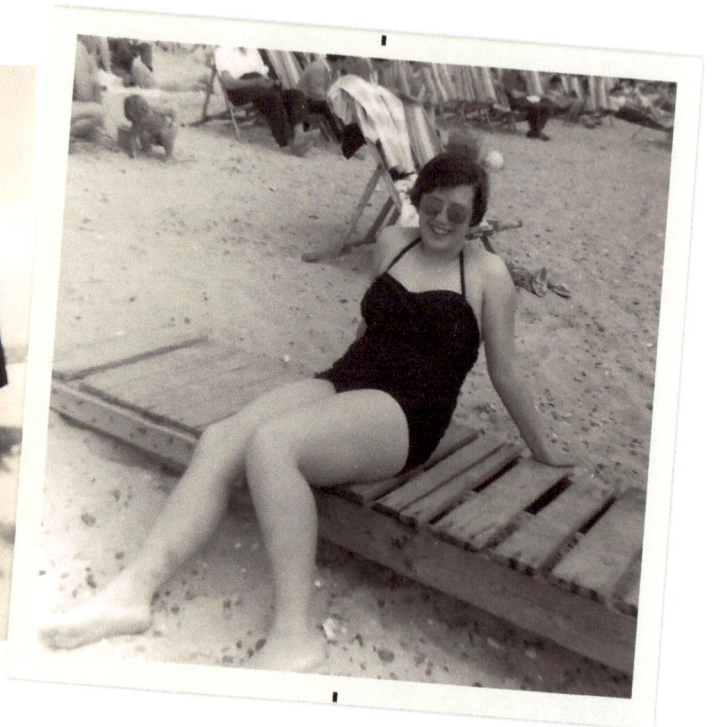

On beach at Great Yarmouth, aged 2 and 13.

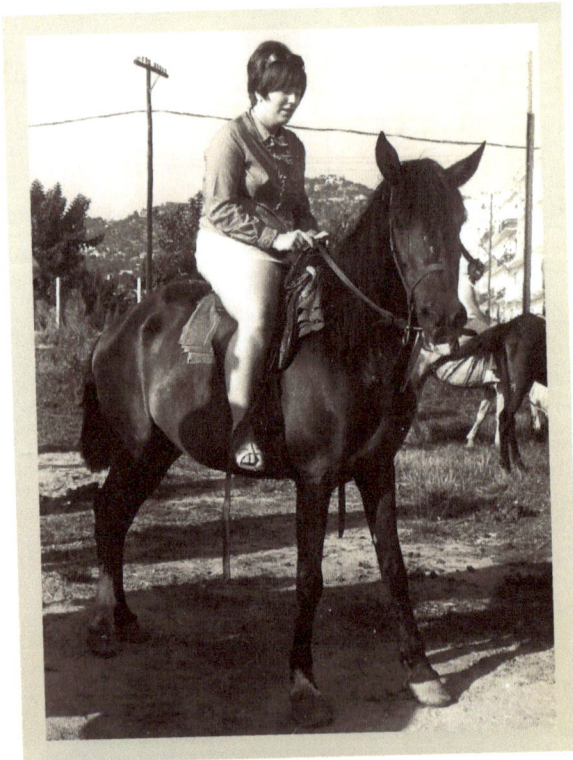

Me on "Nijinsky" in Benidorm.

early 1970s, it was the fashion to wear hair extensions. My roommate, Ann, took hers together with the white polystyrene head that she used to pin it on to style. Our room was on about the third floor and after a

night out we decided to tie some string (you always took string to peg out your cossie on the balcony) around the head and dangle it over the balcony. We laid on the floor in hysterics hearing the screams of the people coming in late and a bit tipsy as they bashed into the head.

On another trip with Ann the group decided to go horse riding. Well coming from Bethnal Green you never even saw a horse let alone ride one. Plus I never possessed a pair of trousers so there I was in this skirt on a horse. As I knew nothing about horseback riding I didn't realise that the stirrups had to be at the right height for your feet for you to grip the horse. Mine weren't and all along these stirrups were banging into my ankles. Ann and I were terrified and so slow that the guide kept hitting our horses to make them go faster. Halfway round the tour we stopped for a drink and going back to the horses found that someone had taken ours and left us with the biggest horses imaginable. We nearly died on the spot but had no choice. Luckily we only had a short journey back to the stables. The next day I could hardly walk as both my ankles were swollen and covered in bruises.

In Denia I have found a new family. Janet worked

Denia, Spain c. 1985.

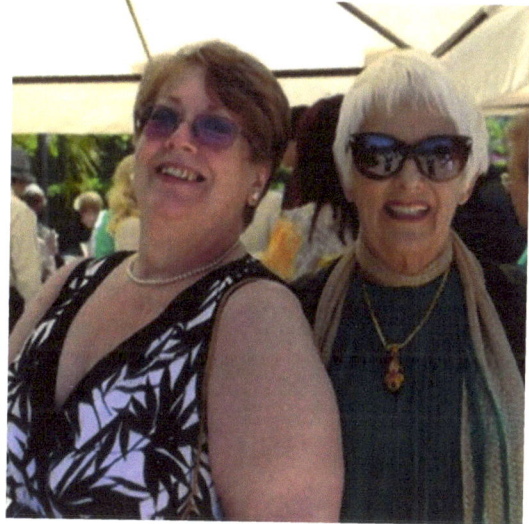

with my Mum in the 1950s and they stayed friends right up until Mum died. In appreciation of the things my Mum did for her, Janet would let Pam and I stay in one of her villas on the beach and then when her husband died we would stay in her magnificent villa in the mountains. She has a wonderful son, daughter and grandchildren and they treat me as one of their own. Over the years I have spent many holidays in Denia, firstly with family and more recently with my friend Pam.

No talk of holidays could go by without the mention of the frequent visits to see family in America.

My first trip to America was in 1988 when Mum, Daniel, Sally and I made a trip to Disneyland. Going all that way we decided to first visit my cousin Alma, her husband and children in a small town called Mission, just outside Vancouver. On one of our

Denia, Janet and me.

sightseeing visits into Vancouver, I happened to mention that a graduate student I had known at the LSE was a Member of Parliament in Canada. What a coincidence that he was the Member for Vancouver.

Me in Rome during Sally and my cruise. Gosh it was hot and I do love a walk!

We went to a phone box and looked up his office number but his secretary said he was in Ottawa on Parliament business. I mentioned how I knew him and gave my cousin's landline number if he remembered me. By the time we arrived back home he had already called but did call again and we had a lovely chat. From Canada we went to Los Angeles and I remember on arriving at the airport Daniel noticed that people would just abandon their trolleys with the coins still left in them. He was running around all over the place putting the trolleys back and pocketing the money.

Our next trip was the early 1990s when Mum, Sally and I went to Jenifer and John's wedding. Talk about travelling style, we went from the house to the church

in a stretch limousine, the first and last time I had been in one.

In 1996 Harris, Pearl's husband, had rented two adjoining houses in Cape Cod to celebrate Pearl's sixtieth birthday. It was wonderful just spending time with so much family. In England there was just Mum, me, Daniel, Sally and Harry, my brother. In America there were four cousins, various spouses and multiple second cousins.

In 1997 Mum, Sally and I spent Christmas and New Year In Medway again, with all the family. We drove around the streets looking at all the decorations, which was way before they became popular here.

I was back again in 2003, this time with my aunt's friend, Alice. I had known Alice for many years

Me and the wonderful Alice.

but never had that much to do with her before this trip. Although she had a flat in Snaresbrook her job working for the Foreign Office took her all around the world. When we landed in Boston, Pearl and Harris were there to meet us holding up to signs. You know the kind where car drivers wait to pick up their rides. One read Duchess of Chingford the other Countess of Woodford. How embarrassing.

This was a wonderful trip as they had arranged for us all to travel down the east coast from Medway to Savannah. Harris hired a big van and he and Pearl did the driving. Our route included Atlantic City, Williamsburg, Charleston and then onto Harris' brother David who lived in Savannah. To get to David's house we would cross Moon River named after the song by Johnny Mercer who was born there. He died in 1976 and we visited his burial spot in the historic Bonaventure Cemetery (thanks Google).

During the trip my Aunt was complaining of a lot of back pain and it eventually turned out she had bladder cancer. By the time she had been diagnosed it had metastasised but she said she was okay but I made a trip out on my own the following year to see her. Unfortunately she died in June 2005.

In 2011 Sally and I went on a Mediterranean cruise.

Two women in one cabin for two weeks does not work as there's not enough space for all your clothes. I have never taken part in so many quizzes or played so many games of deck shuffleboard in my life. This was supposed to be a nice relaxing holiday. I took five books away with me to read and relax and ended up reading one paragraph of the first book I picked up. Sally was having none of my protests replying, "Mother, you are retired, you can read when you get home". I got my own back though. At one of the quizzes that we attended after dinner there was a question of tv music themes. One of the answers was Ski Sunday and you could get an extra point if you could act out the music. Sally said "Don't you dare" but I couldn't resist. There I was, up the front in my posh evening dress, performing as if I was on skis.

Some of my American cousins have been to visit in England but my last trip out west was in March 2018 and a gift from Daniel and Sally for my seventieth birthday. Sally and I travelled Business Class (poor

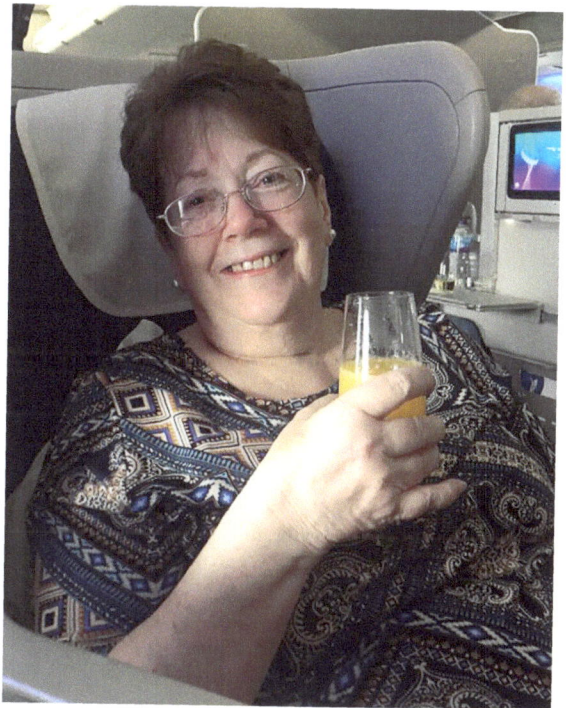

Travelling to Boston, Business Class, a treat for my 70th birthday from my children.

Mark in economy) and that whole package was an experience in itself. Breakfast before boarding and my own television screen. Although Sally thought it was quite funny to press buttons to lay me out flat and then raise the screen between us so that I was stuck. But she did put me in the aisle so I could annoy the cabin crew instead of her.

I had the most wonderful time and was able to catch up again on my wonderful family. They even arranged a belated birthday party and cake.

After some of the Covid restrictions were lifted Sally, Mark, his brother George, his Dad Ken, stepmum Lorraine and I rented two bungalows in Cornwall. On the first day we all did a lateral flow test, just to be on the safe side, and went about our business while they were "cooking". Mark and his Dad went to get some shopping and luckily all the tests came back negative but us girls decided to have a bit of fun and draw an extra red line on mine. When they came back and took a look, they saw that one was "positive", found out it was mine and sent me to my bedroom while Mark was in a total panic trying to find somewhere that did a PCR test. Sally and Lorraine had to leave the room to stop them laughing out loud. Even when we told him later he wouldn't believe us. ♠

EARNING A CRUST

I WAS NEVER one of those people to have a Saturday job although I remember working at a dry cleaners in Bethnal Green Road called Attaboys for a week during a half term. At the end of the first day my feet were killing me so much that I couldn't walk for the rest of the day. During another half term I did a stint at a tie manufacturer near Old Street and was put on the switchboard. It was a nightmare and it was only on my last day that I cracked it.

My first proper job on leaving school in 1965 was for the boss of a company called Blunt & Wray in Clerkenwell Road, part of the Pollard Group, that made church furnishings. The boss didn't just speak, he bellowed and it made me very nervous so after a couple of months I contacted Personnel (now Human Resources) to say I wanted to leave. As they didn't want to lose me they offered me a job in another of their companies called Haskins, which was in St John Street. They manufactured "up and over garage doors". It was so boring just typing estimates all day and this at a time when there were no computers. If you made a mistake you would have to insert a piece of correction tape over the error, type the wrong letter again and then take it out and type in the correct letter.

Years later, after Pam had stayed the weekend, we were going to work on the bus and as we got to St John Street she told me that she had worked there at a company called Pollards. I said I had too. She then said she had worked for Haskins and I said I had too. Apparently the job I had taken had been hers and I had sat in her chair, at her desk.

I didn't stay there very long and moved onto a building company called Holborn Management in Chancery Lane, right opposite the Prudential Building which actually shone pink in the rain. Although I started off typing I found my forte in doing bookkeeping. My boss at that time was Richard Deterding who, I believe, was a bit of a manic depressive. He hated the Prudential Building and, as we were on the sixth floor, would shoot fireworks at it.

I worked for them for about 9 years and then joined The London School of Economics. This job was in one of their Halls of Residence in Endsleigh Place, Passfield Hall, just off Tavistock Square. I loved this job and I felt I was like a mother to 177 students. I would chase them up for unpaid fees and if they hadn't changed their sheets. During holiday times the hall ran as a hotel so there was a lot of interaction with the public. I stayed friends with two of the students, Kaiyan Kaikobad, who became a lecturer but sadly died in 2010, and Nilesh Dattani, who is a lecturer at the LSE.

I was delighted when they both came to visit me

in Chingford during the 1980s. They arrived at Chingford Station and were so busy in conversation that they didn't realise they had reached their destination. The guard, on checking the train, found them and asked them if they hadn't heard the announcement and couldn't they understand English. These two chaps had more brains in their little fingers than the guard had in his whole body. Luckily they saw the funny side.

I left Passfield Hall in September 1978 when I was pregnant with Daniel.

Around 1994/5 when the business wasn't doing too well I started working for friends, John and Monica, at first part time and then full time. Never work for friends. We never knew what mood John would be in the morning and Monica liked to lord it over everyone. Although I was a bookkeeper she liked to keep me in my place by sending me to sort out files while her son sat in the corner playing patience on his computer. By January 1997 I had had enough and left.

Just after that I got a job working for a company called Negs Photographic owned by Jim and Doreen Holloway. Their studio was in Broadwick Street, Soho but their accounts etc were carried out in their house in Loughton. What a difference in bosses. We were like family, I even dog sat when they went on holiday. I had never done accounts work on a computer but even surprised myself how quickly I picked it up. Who said you can't teach an old dog new tricks.

When they moved house I set up an office in my small front bedroom but eventually they sold the business although I carried on working for the new owner for a time. I don't think he particularly liked

the set up and within a short time he made me redundant. June 2006 was the first time I had ever had to sign on although I did get another job in the October working for another building company who did new build and refurbishments. This was at The Mount, Chingford and the boss had a daughter who was in the same class as Sally at Normanhurst.

By the summer of 2008 the boss, Mr. Smith, decided he wanted to retire so once again I was told I was being made redundant. As he had friends in business he introduced me to an acquaintance who offered me a job at an upmarket joinery company based in Gant's Hill. Unfortunately the work was mainly computer based and not accounts. I remember the first day I was there one of the bosses asked me to write some cheques to pay bills. I then volunteered to write up the cash book. The next day he asked me what a cash book was. I don't know how they ran their business. The family were Sikhs and the father asked me if I would take down a letter and type it up. I had so much trouble understanding his accent that I kept asking him to repeat what he said. He asked me if I was hard of hearing!

I had been doing such a good job getting them to tender for jobs that they had to take on a new quantity surveyor. I was told he would be starting the following Monday but, as I was part time, I would not meet him until Tuesday. On arriving at work on Tuesday not only had he been given my parking spot he was also working at my desk. I left. I wasn't going to be treated like that. Despite many efforts to get me back I decided I quite liked being retired. ♠

MY OLYMPIC DREAM

IN THE SUMMER OF 2011 I completed an application form to become a Gamesmaker at the 2012 Olympics. On 30 August I heard that my application had been successful and that I was invited to attend a selection event and an interview with the Protocol team. I had never heard the word before so had no idea what was involved.

The interview was scheduled for the 22 September at the EXCEL centre and the whole process was quite daunting. On the way home I was chatting to another

2012 London Olympics. Final day of competition with my Gamesmaker colleagues.

candidate and saying how stressed it had been and that I didn't think I would get any further. She must have been having her interview quite close to me and told me I would be alright as I "had the gift of the gab". I just looked it up and the definition means to have the ability to talk glibly and persuasively.

I thought she must have got it wrong and by May 2012 I had forgotten all about it.

On 14 June I received a telephone call from a well spoken man called Patrick Harwood asking if I would like to join his team. I seriously thought he had been asked by my friend Dave as a set up. I listened and then asked if this was a joke. Patrick said no and that he had all my details and that my children were Daniel and Sally. I replied that Dave would know that. Anyway, within an hour he had sent me an email showing that he wasn't pulling my leg and I was on my way. I did ask if there was any chance of David Beckham showing up and he said anything was possible. He never did. I was going to be working in Arena 3 of the EXCEL Centre for Weightlifting – typecast or what. On 5 July I was picking up my uniform and from there I had a series of training days. I was selected to be part of the Protocol team which meant looking after members of the Olympic Family (naively I thought this meant the athletes relations), members of the Weightlifting Federation and dignitaries. We were responsible for the lounge room, making sure the VIPs got to their correct seats and escorting them to present medals.

Three days before the start I was asked to join a few others for an Olympic Broadcast Service dress rehearsal. At the end our Arena Manager Patrick asked us if we would like to take part as medal winners. After some begging and pleading I managed to persuade my colleagues to let me "win" the Gold Medal. I just knew how realistic I could make it as I would definitely have cried when they played the National Anthem.

Three days later it was all systems go. Well it

2012 London Olympics. Me in my Gamesmaker uniform.

would have been if it had been organised properly. There were so many different stations that had to be manned but no rota showing who was to be where. But between us all, at the end of shift, we had it down pat and a list typed up for the rest of the games. From the beginning of the first shift to the end I had the most amazing time.

Nearly every day on my way to "work" somebody on the train would see me in my uniform and ask me what I was doing and take great interest in everything.

I escorted the President of Azerbaijan to the lounge, looked after a female minister when she presented medals and was the only one who recognised Clive Woodward when he was entering the lounge.

While on duty in the main hall I started talking to a gentleman called Patrick Jarvis, who was on the Governing Board of the Canadian International Paralympic Committee and a former Paralympian.

He had just asked me my name when the introductory music started (song by Muse) and he misheard what I said so I repeated a bit louder, Hazel, a reddish brown nut. He laughed. Sometime later, during the Paralympics I met him again as he was rushing off to Stratford. He called out, "Hazel – reddish brown nut".

I was on duty on Super Saturday when Team GB won three gold medals and remember being in the lounge with Bob Neil MP. He wrote us a lovely letter thanking us for the outstanding job we were doing. I even got letters from Lord Coe and David Cameron, Prime Minister at that time.

While the games were on I was lucky to get to see the Hockey and Handball at the Olympic Park and it was while I was there with Daniel I had my very first (and last) McDonalds. I also went to Horse Guards Parade with Sally to see Beach Volleyball.

Our last shift was the 11 August, the next day being the closing ceremony at Stratford. On the morning of the 12th I got a telephone call from Patrick, our Arena Manager, asking me what I was doing later. I informed him that as it was my Mum's birthday – the first without her – I was going to have dinner with Sally and Mark and watch the Closing Ceremony at their house. He replied saying he had been given a ticket by the head of the Weightlifting Federation but as he was on duty could he give it to one of his Gamesmakers. That was me. I couldn't believe it. I had to meet him at Stratford to pick up the ticket and I cried all the way to the station. Mum was looking down on me. When I got to Stratford I borrowed one of those large foam hands with the pointy fingers and pointed it at me

when I saw Patrick coming, so he could find me amongst the crowds. If I hadn't been selected as a member of the Protocol team, I would have loved to have been one of the Gamesmakers sitting on a high chair with a foam hand directing people to the stadiums.

The Closing Ceremony was fantastic. I was sitting on the side, nine rows from the front next to a French man. There were different artists performing, but then Muse appeared and played Survival. The song that had played before every session of the weightlifting. It gave me goosebumps which I happened to mention to the French man. He offered me his jacket thinking I was cold. Talk about lost in translation.

Just over two weeks later I was back at the EXCEL centre this time for Sitting Volleyball for the Paralympics. Same Protocol job but this wasn't as busy or intense and didn't last as long. It was a bit surreal to see the athletes enter the court, take off their prosthetic limbs and have them put in a big wire cage.

On 10 September 2012 there was an Athletes Parade through London and my colleagues and I met up on The Strand. People were coming up to us and thanking us for the job we had done. I felt very proud and honoured to have been part of it all.

After the parade many of us went to The Crypt at St Martins and nearly every year since we have had a reunion at Henry's Bar in Piccadilly. Obviously not in 2020 and 2021 but hopefully if not this year perhaps next. ◉

A NEW LEASE OF LIFE

WHEN I WAS 64 I was accepted to be a Gamesmaker for the 2012 London Olympics where I met so many wonderful people which gave me the confidence to start a singing class. I had first seen the advert in the local paper in 2013 to join a class called Singing the Musicals. I loved musicals and had seen so many shows but it took me another year to pluck up the courage to join. It gave me a new lease of life. During our final term Jenny, our teacher, allowed us to pick a song and sing in front of family and friends. I was so nervous but was able to belt out Cilla Black's You're My World. My daughter even bought me a bouquet of flowers. I felt like a right diva.

From there the teacher asked if I would like to join one of her other classes at Enfield Civic and then I joined another of her classes. We sang at festivals for Chingford a few times and Enfield. The choirs were made up mainly of women, with a few men popping in and out. My favourite venue was the Walled Gardens at Valentines Park. On one particular occasion I was asked to sing Oh! Carol by Neil Sedaka but it didn't seem right that I should sing about another woman, so my daughter suggested I take a very large two sided photo of David Beckham and when it came to the speaking part I would talk to it.

Only the teacher knew what I was going to do but it did give everyone a laugh.

One of our last "gigs" was supposed to be a film of us singing a Queen song for promotional purposes. First of all we recorded one of their songs at a recording studio and then we went to Victoria Station where we were going to shoot the video. Don't really know what happened but none of it materialised. Fame had again passed me by.

Sadly COVID has put the singing classes on hold.

Around 2015 my friend Linda Burrell started to look for girls she had started school with in 1959. In June she found Elka, her first victim, and in September that year there was a reunion at the school (which is now Central Foundation) and arranged to meet up. Several others of us were in attendance and from there it grew. She has since tracked down between 40 and 50 and we call ourselves the 59ers (we all started senior school in 1959) and we would regularly meet in Stratford for lunch. Due to ill health some can't join us, some have died but only one has rebutted her contact. Her loss. During Covid we set up Zoom meetings. One of our group lives in Australia and one in France but many of us have stayed relatively close to home. ●

ANECDOTES

I HAVE ADDED LITTLE STORIES that have stayed with me over the years.

After meeting Eileen on the trip to Rome and Cattolica we'd often meet for lunch but not much more – I was only 17 and she was a bit older and quite streetwise. I had never been to a club up the West End and she wanted me to go to a club called Le Kilt somewhere off Oxford Street. I got the okay from my Mum, which surprised me, but many years later she informed me that she had telephoned the West End police to see if it was safe for me to go.

Every week during my teens my school friend Christine and I would go to a local cinema. On one such occasion the ice cream lady approached us and offered us an ice cream from a gentleman a few rows back. This kind of thing wasn't allowed as you never knew what you were going to get yourself into. It turned out the gentleman a few rows back was the Travel Officer for the Supporters Club and probably four times my age.

I sometimes went to Leyton Orient with my friend Carol. Being a small football club everyone knew everyone and that included the players. I believe one game was on my birthday and a few of us, including some of the players, went back to mine. My Mum and Dad were there and we played music and chatted. All of a sudden one of the players started to do a striptease to the music. I thought my parents would be furious but instead everyone thought it was hilarious. That player was David Webb who went on to play for Chelsea and manage Southend United, amongst others.

Some football supporters have quite a good sense of humour. In the 1970s Tottenham had a winger called Ralph Coates and during one game one of the crowd encouraged him to cross the ball from the wing to the penalty area shouting out "over Coates". A retort came back "mackintoshes".

During the 1970s my Dad worked for a company called 4S Sports and he used to travel abroad for all different kinds of sports events. I went with him to Paris to see the Prix de l'arc de Triomphe and to Berlin for an England match. On the journey home from one European Football trip to Greece with Leeds United fans the noisy plane fell silent when one of the propellers shut off. All of a sudden one comedian started to sing "We're on our way to heaven, we shall not be moved".

Always being up for a bit of a laugh, I once went to a fancy dress party and halfway through the evening changed into a gorilla outfit I had rented. My friend John and I went out into the street but he wouldn't get on a bus with me so we settled on going to a nearby mini cab office. Still can't understand

Me in fancy dress at a party
held in De Vere Gardens c. 1977.

Janet and Brian's
fancy dress party 1974.

why there was a stampede to lock the door.

Shortly after Alan and I moved to Ilford we decided to install central heating. As it was winter time we stayed with my Mum and Nan while the work was being done. Alan had had a false eye since very young and would put it on my Nan's mantelpiece before going to bed. The next day Honey, the dog, could be heard crunching on a pear dropped by Alan as he was always eating them, at least that's what we thought. But what had really happened was one of the cats had climbed onto the mantelpiece, started playing with the eye which made it fall on the floor and in the evening Honey had found it.

Whilst working at Passfield Hall one of the students would act as caretaker over the Christmas holidays. During the Christmas period of 1977 Kaiyan had this job as all his family were in Pakistan and he couldn't make the journey home. We invited him to spend Christmas Day with us and Alan and I drive to Euston to pick him up. During a conversation he was

telling us about his family and that he came from a region near the Khyber Pass. He couldn't understand why we fell into fits of laughter until we told him that Khyber Pass was rhyming slang for an intimate part of the body.

During the early 1990s my friends, Beryl, Bet, Joy and I went to see Gene Pitney at the London Palladium. In the first half there was a comedian as the warm up. He came down into the audience and picked out four gentlemen to go up on stage. He then came down again looking for four women and from the first two he picked up I knew he was looking for a particular type and they weren't slim. He got to me and, with my friends egging me on, I went up on stage. It turned out he wanted the men to lay on the floor and the women to stand on their back. I turned to the gentleman I was paired with and told him to follow my lead. I lay on the floor and he stood on my back. I think I got more laughs than the comedian.

On Sundays some men would go out for a drink,

come home to eat their dinner and then have an afternoon nap. One particular Sunday afternoon Queen Mary was in the East End and knocked at the door of one of my Grandad's drinking buddies' prefab house on the side of the Regent's Canal in Bethnal Green. His wife quickly ran to the bedroom and told her husband to get up as Queen Mary was there and he replied "How the bloody hell did they get that big ship up the Canal?".

I have been trying to rack my brains when it was, but one of the best Christmas presents I received was for one of those Red Letter Days bought by Sally (probably her idea) and Daniel. It was a two hour recording session in a studio in Brixton. I thought I could make an album in two hours. What do I know?! I had selected the Power of Love by Jennifer Rush as my first song and on arrival our host started to play the tune. I didn't even recognise it. It was just the music and nothing like karaoke which I was expecting.

I had no idea when to come in so the engineer had to play the original song through my headphones so I could follow. After the first take I motioned to Sally how did it sound and she pulled a face. Oh dear. No way was I going to be making an album. After several takes the engineer put together the best bits and hey presto I now have my very own CD.

Some things you may not know about me.

1. *I have never worn or owned a pair of jeans.*
2. *I can't stand ticking clocks.*
3. *I never went into a proper restaurant until I was 22.*
4. *I always eat the top of a roll, scone or hot cross bun first cause I like the bottom the best.*
5. *I have never ordered a takeaway.*
6. *I never go out without wearing my perfume or pearl earrings.*
7. *I never regret anything. You can't change it so don't regret it.* ◉

BUCKET LIST

ABOUT 10 YEARS AGO I decided to write a bucket list. I have been extremely lucky to do most of them but, alas, I think Nos. 1, 8 and 9 are outstanding and are unlikely to happen.

1. Meet David Beckham
2. Go to Lords Cricket Ground
3. Go to the Oval Cricket Ground
4. Go on Eurostar
5. Go to a rugby match at Twickenham
6. Go to a Formula 1 Grand Prix
7. Go on the Emirates Cable Car
8. Throw the javelin
9. Toss the shot putt
10. Get a tattoo

1
DAVID BECKHAM

I always thought what a nice, down to earth chap he was and my love of football and both of us having connections with Chingford we'd have a bit in common. Sally always said that if I was on my death bed she would try and get him to come and see me. You see that kind of thing all the time on the news. But I didn't want him to see me at my worst so thought I would write him a letter. No luck I'm afraid.

May 2014

Dear David Beckham,

I am 66 years old, have a bucket list and meeting you is at the top of it. My daughter did say that if I was ever really ill and in hospital, she would have written to you then but I feel it would be preferable to meet you while I still have all my marbles.

So, I was wondering if I could treat you to pie and mash sometime?

To prove I am not a nutcase I have been CIB checked as I was a Games Maker at the 2012 Olympics. In fact when I was asked to be part of the Protocol Team for Weightlifting by my Arena Manager, Patrick Harwood, I did ask if there was any chance you would pay a visit. He did say that by working for him anything was possible but, alas, the nearest I got was when he met you and shook your hand at the Beach Volleyball. I attach the e-mail that he sent out.

Further proof is that my son-in-law's father, Ken Slade, used to play football with your Dad and you actually played a game of pool with my son-in-law, Mark, at Wadham Lodge.

I promise you that I will not tell anyone of a possible meeting (even my children) if you could make this happen, and if you preferred I could get the pie and mash and we could have it at mine.

You don't need a chaperone (!) but feel free to bring anyone with you.

I watched you on the Only Fools and Horses sketch for Sport Relief and you intimated that doing it was a dream come true for you, so how about making a dream come true for me?

Yours sincerely,

Hazel Lewis

2 & 3
LORDS AND OVAL CRICKET GROUNDS

Me with David "Bumble" Lloyd.

I have now done this and, in fact, have been to The Oval twice. The second time was the best. The President of the cricket club that Daniel plays for, Paul Newman, writes for the Daily Mail and sometimes ghost writes for David (Bumble) Lloyd.

Well, if I couldn't meet David Beckham, Bumble would make a wonderful substitute. We arranged to do hospitality, which could also go on a bucket list on its own, and that we would meet him during the lunch break.

We were standing in a passageway waiting for Paul to bring him when all of a sudden he appeared behind me. All of a sudden, me, a person who could talk for England, am struck dumb. Afterwards, I could've kicked myself. I do have a lovely photo to show for it.

4
GO ON EUROSTAR

In September 2019 I approached a few of my closest 59ers to see if they would be interested in making a trip to the Lille Christmas Market in early December. It was all booked for the first week in December and then on the 2 December I got laryngitis and a chest infection and couldn't go. Subsequently Sally bought us two tickets for my Christmas present and we went in February 2020.

Getting ready to travel to Lille on Eurostar.

5
GO TO A RUGBY MATCH
AT TWICKENHAM

One day in early November 2013 Daniel phoned me from work asking if I had any plans for the weekend as he was going to come over to watch the rugby with me. This was a ruse just to make sure I didn't have any plans as he had bought two tickets for us to go and see England v Argentina.

I loved it but the only complaint was that people would be in and out going to the toilet. That doesn't happen at football matches.

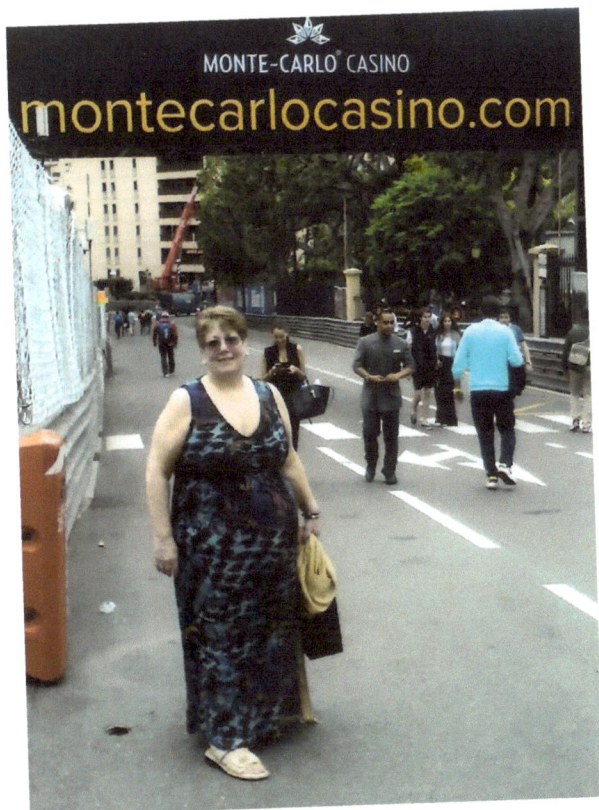

Monaco Grand Prix.

6
GO TO A FORMULA 1
GRAND PRIX

In 2015, and completely out of the blue, a very dear friend sent me a cheque for £5,000. I didn't want to just put it in the bank and gradually whittle it away so decided to treat myself. I decided on a hospitality trip to a F1 motor race and off Daniel and I went to Monaco. The money paid for the flights and package and I found a really cheap hotel in Nice. We only needed somewhere to sleep.

It was a fantastic experience and now I just need to win the Lottery to be able to go to Abu Dhabi.

7
GO ON THE EMIRATES CABLE CAR

This is the next objective and I and the Golden Girls hope to go this summer.

8 & 9
THROW THE JAVELIN AND
TOSS THE SHOT PUTT

I think I am going to have to pass on this. Old age and Covid has got in the way.

10
GET A TATTOO

This has been achieved. I have a tiny heart with the initials D and S in the middle, obviously for Daniel and Sally. I did tell them if they upset me I'll have Nintendo added. Sally called it my tramp stamp. 🌰

*Daniel at the
Monaco Grand Prix on our way to the Casino.*

MY SEVENTIES

JANUARY 2018, my seventieth year, started off with a bang and I've got to say, when I put on a party I put on a party.

I rented a hall in South Chingford for over sixty people and, even if I say so myself, it was one hell of a night. We had a live singer, sixties dance songs, plenty of drinks and all the food you could eat. And the ladies from my signing class joined me on stage to sing a few songs. Couldn't have done it without Anita, Christine, Karen, Pam, Sharon,

Laura, Daniel, me, Sally and Mark. Seventieth Birthday.

Entertaining the crowd at my seventieth birthday party. L-r Sharon, Karen, Sue, Anita, me, Pam, Christine, Yetundi, Shirley Anne and our entertainer for the evening Max Curto. Who also performed at Sally's wedding.

Shirley-Ann, Sue, Yetunid and Jenny our teacher. The highlight, of course, was me singing Cilla Black's You're My World. In the days following I had girls saying they could hardly talk the next day and that their feet were killing them. Sign of a good party. One person even offered to pay her share if I would put on another.

Life carried on as normal but who would have thought that two years later the whole world would be turned upside down.

Life under COVID was horrendous. No going out, not even to the supermarket – all my food was delivered. All live sport on the television was cancelled and no soaps. One good thing was that the weather was extremely good that March and having such good neighbours to chat over the fence was a life saver. I would listen to Gold on the radio a lot and sing

Neighbours from Crescent Road, Jill and John Crafer. Seventieth Birthday.

Golden Girls at lunch March 2022. Me, Glenis, Pat, Elka, Barbara and Sue.

along. Plus, I could easily get a job with Border Force, as I know all the tricks that the crooks try to pull. I even got fed up with watching Judge Judy but would sit with her programme on the television with the sound off just so it was like someone was in the room with me.

As things got a little easier Sally would come and sit in the garden. Luckily my house is what they call tunnel linked so she didn't have to come through the house. Another one of my friends, Barbara, who loves walking, came over one day having to do a ten mile round trip.

When life became a little easier and we could go out, I still wouldn't go into a supermarket although I would venture to my lovely butcher, Andy, who could put a smile on anyone's face. Although, I had this terrible feeling that this terrible virus would put its hand on my shoulder one day and say "Gotcha".

Life is still not normal now and I wonder if it ever will but at least plans can be made. The 59ers has

My best friend Pam at my seventieth birthday party.

shrunk to six Golden Girls for the time being and its lovely meeting up with Glenis (who I have known since I was 4 at nursery) Pat and Barbara for 69 years and Elka and Sue who I met in 1959.

And since starting writing I have now had COVID but thanks to the vaccinations it's not the deadly virus for us old folks that it used to be.

And finally, of course, Catherine Grace who came into my life in 2021. It all worked out in the end. ♠

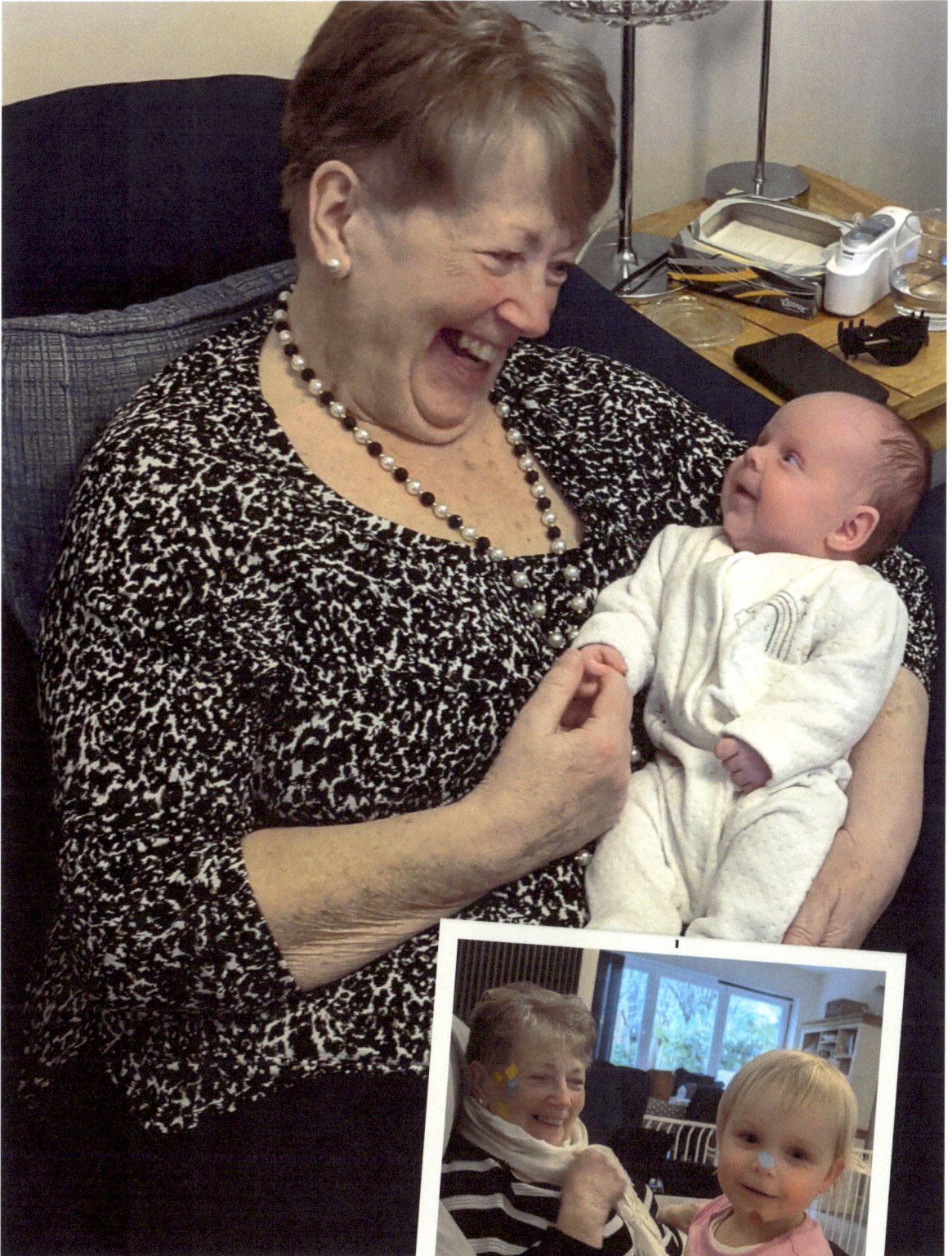

Catherine and me, November 2021 her first smile.

February 2024.

EPILOGUE

I KNOW ONCE I HAVE COMPLETED this book I will remember things I'd forgotten and want to kick myself but that would be a regret and I don't do regrets.

Other than my two children the greatest gift in my life has been my friends. I may not have mentioned all of them in this book but I appreciate their friendships and know that if ever I needed help they would be there for me. What more could anyone ask for. ◉

www.ingramcontent.com/pod-product-compliance
Lightning Source LLC
Chambersburg PA
CBHW042004100426
42813CB00020B/2974